NorthParadePublishing

©2018 North Parade Publishing Ltd.
4 North Parade,
Bath BA11LF. UK
Printed in China.
www.nppbooks.co.uk

coral

fashion

plant

pyramid

bat

frog

Picture Encyclopedia

hawk

A Complete Pictorial Guide to the World

Contents

THE UNIVERSE

Universal Universe!

How do you define universe? The Universe is the sum total of everything that exists — the space and everything in it ¬— all matter and energy, the planets, the moons, the stars, the galaxies, asteroids, anything and everything that you can think of.

Big Bang!

The 'Big Bang' theory is the most common and well-known theory about the origin of the universe. Proponents of the theory believe that around 10 – 20 billion years ago, a massive blast occurred which led to the creation of the universe – matter and energy sprung from some ancient form of energy.

Larger than the largest!

Richard Got III and Mario Jurice along with a team of astronomers have discovered a huge wall of galaxies which is supposedly the largest structure in the universe. Do you know how long this wall is? This wall is 1.37 billion light-years long (9.4 trillion kilometres make one light year)! Their amazing discovery was announced in 2003.

Asteroid or Dwarf Planet?

As you may already know, there is an asteroid belt between Mars and Jupiter. The largest asteroid in this belt is Ceres which has a diameter of 941 kilometres. And do you know when Ceres was discovered? Ceres was discovered on 1st January 1801 in Sicily by Giuseppe Piazzi. Ceres is not only the largest asteroid but it is also known as the smallest dwarf planet! Amazing how one thing can be largest and smallest at the same time!

I am the largest!

Scientists don't really agree with each other on this one, but it is generally believed that the largest star is VY Canis Majoris, a red supergiant, some 5000 light years away from the Earth! The diameter of the star is estimated to be between 2.5 and 3 billion kilometres. Scientists claim that if VY Canis Majoris is placed in the centre of the solar system, its outer surface would reach beyond the orbit of Jupiter!

One universe or many?

This has been an ongoing debate for many years and it will continue for years to come. Many scientists believe that the universe that we live in is just one universe. There are many more in existence. Michio Kaku, a theoretical physicist at the City College of New York calls is the concept of 'multiverse'. He explains that each universe is like a bubble and "the multiverse is like a bubble bath," with "multiple universes bubbling, colliding and budding off each other" all the time. Whether it is true or not, only time will tell.

STARS AND GALAXIES

Of stars and galaxies!
Stars are nothing but luminous gas, mostly hydrogen and helium. They generate light which is why we can see them. Galaxies are a group of billions of stars that are held together by gravitational forces. Galaxies are generally spiral or elliptical, but there are exceptions too – some galaxies are irregular in shape.

Bigger than our Milky Way!
If you ever thought that Milky Way, our very own galaxy, is too big, wait until you read this. The central galaxy of the Abell 2029 galaxy cluster, which was discovered in 1990, has a diameter of 5.6 million light years which is 80 times the diameter of our Milky Way! 1,070 light years away, this galaxy gives out light which is around two trillion times more than the Sun's light. Distant competition, isn't it?

Of spiral galaxies!
The largest spiral galaxy is Malin 1. It is named after Anglo-Australian astronomer David Malin whose photographs proved the existence of this galaxy in 1986. Malin 1 is 1.1 billion light years away and measures 650,000 light years across – it is so huge that there is no point comparing it to our Milky Way. And did you know that Malin 1 has some 50 billion suns' worth of hydrogen?

Black holes!

When stars bigger than the Sun (about fifteen to twenty times bigger) collapse into themselves, they leave behind a massive burned out remnant. The surface gravity of these remnants is so strong that even light cannot escape its gravitational pull. That begs the question – how do we see them if light cannot escape them? The answer is that when a small black hole passes by a normal star, it pulls some matter towards it. Between this pull and the crashing of this new matter into the black hole, some atoms get charged and emit x-rays. This is how scientists study black holes!

Bright is might!

If we count the Sun out (due to its proximity to the Earth it will always appear brightest), the brightest star as seen from Earth is Sirius, also known as the dog star. It is 24 times brighter than the Sun. The brightest star of the galaxy is Cygnus OB2-12 which is six million times brighter than the sun, but Cygnus cannot be seen from the Earth.

So far, yet so visible!

How far can the naked eye see? A few kilometres, you would think. But the fact is that naked eye can see the Andromeda Galaxy which is 2,309,000 light years away from the Earth! It is visible to the naked eye because it is so huge – it has a diameter of 180,000 light years and has over 300 billion stars. You wouldn't believe it, but the light that we see from Andromeda left the galaxy when the first human appeared on Earth. That's how far it is!

SUN AND SOLAR SYSTEM

Guess my age!

Can you guess how old the solar system is? The solar system was formed 4,560 million years ago! The solar system comprises the planets – Mercury, Venus, Earth, Mars, Jupiter, Saturn, Uranus, Neptune – and their satellites (commonly called moons), comets, and other bodies. The force of gravity keeps all the planets and other bodies together.

The tenth planet?

In the January of 2005, scientists at the Palomar Observatory, led by Mike Brown, spotted a rocky object at the farthest part of the solar system. They named it Xena and called it the tenth planet. Later studies showed that Xena (now officially named Eris), much like Pluto, is a dwarf planet and even slightly bigger than Pluto. Eris has one moon called Dysnomia.

Sunny Sun!

Do you know how far the Sun is from us? Around 149, 597, 893 kilometres away! And hard as it may be to believe, the Sun is more than 100 times larger than the Earth – it has a diameter of 1,391,940 kilometres. The Sun's mass alone is around 99.98 per cent of the total mass of everything in the solar system. Now that is too many feats for one body!

Hot as hell!

That's a saying, but no one knows how hot they mean! What we for a fact is that the hottest place in the solar system is the very centre of the Sun. It is estimated that temperature in the centre of the Sun is at least 15, 600, 000°C and the pressure is at least 250 billion times higher than what we experience at sea level. What would surprise you is the fact that these two reasons make the Sun shine!

Solar system tornado!

Tornado in the solar system? Hard to believe, but it is true. In 1998, scientists observed tornado-like storms on the surface of the Sun. These observations were made with the help of the SOHO satellite. These storms generally occur near the poles of the Sun and are as big as the size of the Earth.

Nearest to the Sun!

What went nearest to the Sun? And how near is near? In 1976, Helios 2, an unmanned spacecraft, got as close as 43.5 million kilometres from the Sun. NASA has created another spacecraft called the Solar Probe+ which will be launched in 2015 and is expected to get as close as 6.2 million kilometres to the Sun!

COMETS, METEORS AND ASTEROIDS

Hail Halley!

Did you know that before Edmond Halley published it, we didn't know that comets travelled in orbits? Halley (1656–1742) told the world that comets travel in orbits, and so calculating their return was possible. He claimed that the comet that he saw in 1682 would return in 1759. Though Halley had died long before 1759, the comet did return and scientists named the comet in his honour – Halley's comet.

How often?

Scientists have estimated that an asteroid larger than 0.4 kilometres hits our Earth every 50,000 years (smaller, inconsequential ones keep coming more often). In fact, scientists believe that one such asteroid that hit our Earth 65 million years ago, killed all the dinosaurs. Whether it is true or false, is difficult to say! In 1991, an asteroid came very close to the Earth but missed by 170,600 kilometres. Another one will pass by in 2050 and will miss by 119,678 kilometres. Let's hope they keep missing their target!

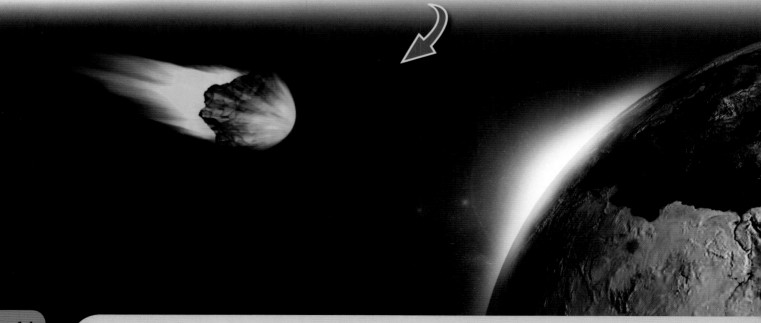

...nat the Guinness Book ...meone the record for ...he maximum number of ...,125! And did you also know ...he only human whose remains ...nd on the moon? He was geologist Eugene Shoemaker, an expert on planetary collisions. His ashes were carried to the Moon aboard NASA's Lunar Prospector. It was crashed into a crater on the Moon on 31st July 1999.

enter the atmosphere of the Earth, they are called meteors; and if any part of it is left behind on the surface of the Earth, it is called a meteorite.

Meteor shower!

Take your sleeping bag outside and lie there with your eyes wide open. You will definitely see one or two meteors falling every few hours. When lots of meteors decide to enter the Earth's atmosphere together, it is called a meteor shower. The direction in which they come from is called a radiant.

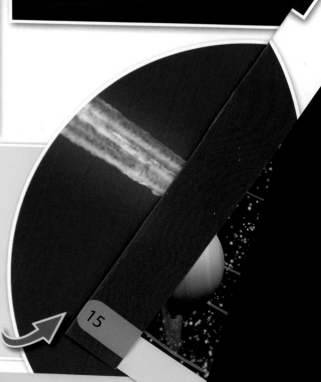

Meteor!

What is a meteor? A meteor is a particle – it could be as small as a grain of sand or as big as a baseball – in space, which burns up on entering the Earth's atmosphere. The larger ones can be bits broken off from asteroids. In outer space, they are called meteoroids; when they

THE BEGINNING

Bang!

Bang! That is how it started. Some five billion years ago, a star exploded and threw out enormous quantities of gas and dust which eventually collided with other clouds of dust. So much energy heated things up and dust began to form clusters. Smaller clusters led to bigger clusters and then all these clusters formed one lump. Gradually, this lump became so hot in the centre (almost 15,600,000°C) that it started generating its own energy. That lump is now called the Sun. The immense heat and the pressure (almost 250 billion times that at sea level on Earth) causes nuclear fusion and that's why the Sun shines.

Getting bigger!

The Sun eventually grew bigger and bigger and the dust that did not become a part of the Sun revolved around it making a disc. Millions of years passed, and these dust particles cooled and first gathered to make grains, then lumps, then boulders and eventually small planet balls – 'embryos' of the planets that we know today. Did you know that like the planets, the Sun too orbits around the centre of our galaxy? It takes 225–250 million years to complete one orbit!

Getting better!

Slowly, but steadily, these 'embryos' developed and organised themselves at distances from the sun. The ones that were close to the Sun found their surfaces scorched by the heat. Depending on the distance from the Sun, the planets receive different amounts of sunlight and heat. Our Earth found a comfortable third spot and has been there ever since.

The coming of the Moon

The planets had been formed but rocks and boulders kept hitting the planets. They would crash into the planets and sometimes parts of the planets would break off and be thrown into space. One such explosion many 'moons' ago, caused a part of the Earth to break off, which the scientists believe forms our moon. Why do scientists think so? Because the rocks that make our moon are so similar to the rocks that make our Earth.

Finally!

The layering of the Earth resulted in tectonic plates and the constant movement of these plates resulted in the formation of mountains and water basins. With these structures in place and ideal conditions – neither too hot nor too cold – our planet was ready to welcome the first forms of life.

The layering!

Whilst all this was happening, the Earth was nothing like the planet that we know today. There was no subdivision of the mantle or core and the Earth was just a huge lump of rock. After millions of years and many collisions, the centre of the Earth became very hot and there was lot of molten rock inside the Earth due to the heat. When the Earth cooled, the core, mantle and crust were formed – the layers that we know of today.

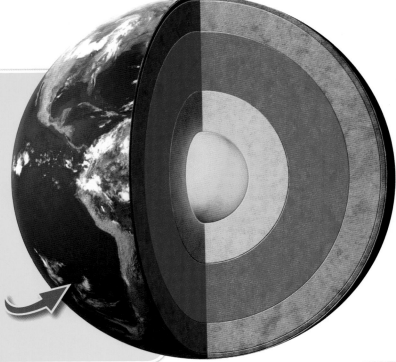

INVERTEBRATES

Invertebrates!

What is an invertebrate? Any creature that doesn't have a vertebra, or spine, is an invertebrate. You would be forgiven for thinking that you haven't seen many creatures without a spine. Wrong! Strange but true, the fact is that 97 per cent of all living organisms are vertebrates! That's correct – an amazing 97 percent!

Same but different!

Well, 97 percent would mean almost everything would be an invertebrate, from the tiny zooplankton to the giant squid! There is so wide a diversity of invertebrates that sometimes they do not share any other characteristic other than the lack of spine. Invertebrates include insects, spiders, worms, snails, centipedes, clams, mussels, jellyfish, squid, and crabs.

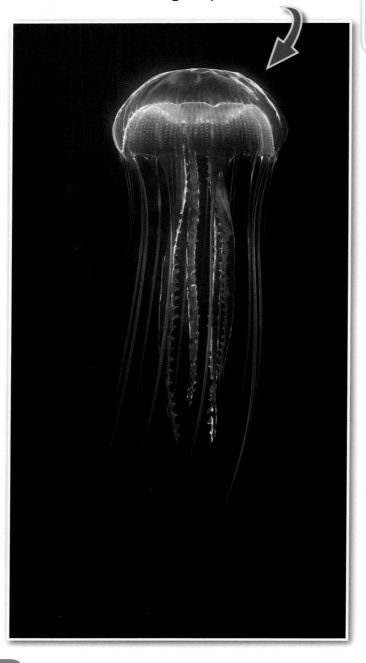

The largest of the largest!

Insects have the distinction of being the largest number of the largest group! Insects do not have a vertebra like all invertebrates. Their body is made of head, thorax, and abdomen. This group is so large that it is difficult to give them a number but scientists estimate that all the insects of the world put together will weigh 12 times more than all the people of the world put together!

Not insects!

Many people thought spiders were insects, did you also think so? Spiders are not insects but belong to a separate group called arachnids. Spiders have four pairs of legs but they do not have wings. Did you know that not all spiders can spin webs, one thing that they are most famous for!

Do you know what beetle means?

Beetle in German means 'little biter'. Beware! Beetles can bite, or so the name suggests! But not all beetles are 'little' some are quite large. In fact, the largest beetle is also the heaviest insect. You guessed it right, it is the goliath beetle. While still a larvae, a goliath beetle can weigh up to 100 grams!

Pedipalps!

These scorpions don't use their pedipalps, commonly called pincers, just for catching prey and digging furrows. These pincers play an important role in mating as well as defence. From its pincer to its stinger, the largest scorpion – one found during World War II in Krishnarajapuram, India – measured a colossal 11.5 inches!

FISH AND OTHER WATER DWELLERS

Why slimy?

Have you ever wondered why fish are so slimy? The slime is nothing more than mucus that fish secrete through their skin. This 'coat of mucus' not only helps fish move through the water faster, it also provides protection against parasites and diseases and also covers any wounds. Some fish also use it as a defence tactic by releasing a toxin in the mucus to ward off predators or attacking creatures while others use their slime to feed their young.

Big fish!

The biggest fish in the world is the whale shark. You probably can't catch this one if you go fishing because, on an average, a whale shark is 12 metres long. There are some exceptions though, such as the one caught off Thailand in 1919 which measured 18 metres. But in spite of their size, whale sharks eat only plankton! Imagine the amount of plankton they would need every day.

Perfect vision!

Fish don't wear spectacles to improve their vision but some of them have special techniques. For example, let's look at the swordfish. It has special organs that heat its eyes up to almost 28°C. This improves their efficiency in cold water and hence, improves the chances of a swordfish spotting and killing prey. What a cool characteristic!

Symbiosis

The goby family is the largest family of marine fish with over 2000 species of this fish! It is difficult for so many of them to stay all together. Most of them form symbiotic relationships with the pistol shrimp. The pistol shrimp has very poor eyesight but makes amazing burrows and the goby is lazy but can see! So the pistol shrimp stays attached to the goby. The shrimp shares its food with the goby and in turn, when danger approaches, the goby alerts the pistol shrimp and the two of them hide in the burrow!

Dangerous delicacy!

The Japanese puffer fish, or maki maki, is an expensive delicacy in Japan, and not everyone can afford to eat it. Now, you must be wondering why it is dangerous? This is because this fish has a powerful nerve poison that can kill you if you eat it? Then how do people eat it? People are specially trained to cook puffers and the dangerous part is removed and the edible part is kept. Statistics show that at least 50 people die in Japan every year due to eating incorrectly prepared puffers.

Changer!

Changer! What else can you call a fish which can change it shape, size and colour at will? And not only that, it can also change its sex at will throughout its adult life. And if you think that's the end of its antics, you are mistaken. It has another interesting habit – some parrotfish make a cocoon from the mucus excreted by an organ on their head and every night they tuck themselves inside the cocoon and enjoy a good night's sleep.

From once to twice

Global warming has changed many things – even the fruiting season of mushrooms! Some, such as the St. George's mushroom have started fruiting twice a year! The normal fruiting season is autumn but due to changes in the temperature and the climate, they have started fruiting in spring as well.

Do fungi help others?

Yes they do. Look at the ghost orchid. Ghost orchids live in a dormant state for a very long time waiting for the right conditions to grow. Now you must be wondering how this plant survives in that state. It is thanks to the fungi in the soil. And in fact, even when they grow, they do not grow leaves. Instead, they continue their symbiotic relationship with fungi throughout their adult life.

The Penicillin Tale

Do you know that one of the most important antibiotics Penicillin is made from the penicillium fungi? And there is another interesting fact about this fungi-derived antibiotic – if it was tested on guinea pigs instead of mice, scientists would have given up their quest for developing this antibiotic. Why? Because penicillin is toxic to guinea pigs. They would not have been cured but died!

PLANTS

Blessing or curse?

It is difficult to say whether this plant is a blessing or a curse? We are talking about the poppy plant. It is this plant that gives us the ill-reputed 'opium'. Opium contains morphine which is used a pain reliever in many medicines – in small doses. When consumed in medicines, it is beneficial. But when consumed as a drug (not a medical drug) it is harmful! It is not only illegal to use it but can also be fatal.

Taste of food!

We all seem to find our food tastes better with onion in and it is used in many dishes worldwide. But as much as we love eating it, we hate to chop it. What happens is that when an onion is cut, it releases a chemical. And to stop our eyes absorbing the irritating chemical, they start watering! What a wonderful defence mechanism we have! And another thing, did you know that the term onion comes from the Latin word 'unionem' which means unity? Now you know why the many layers of the onion are stuck together to form one!

Grow Slow!

Some trees are slow, very slow! Look at the White Cedar. It takes over hundred years to get to a bare minimum height. A certain white cedar in the Great Lakes area of Canada took 155 years to reach a size of 4 inches! That is quite a slow grower, isn't it?

Root cause!

Christmas trees are very special. Santa leaves us our gifts under this tree, but there is another thing that is interesting to know – one of the Christmas trees is also the oldest living tree in the world. How old? Well, researchers believe it is 9550 years old! But it's not the visible part of the tree that is old, but the roots are that old. The stem and trunk live for around 600 years and then fall off. And new ones then grow on the same root system.

Blood in a tree?

Dragon's blood tree. What an interesting name for a tree! Dragon's blood trees belong to the family of dragon trees which are native to the Socotra archipelago near Africa. But why is the 'blood' added to the name? Because when the tree is wounded, a red resin oozes out of it which looks like blood. It is used in medicine, dyes, varnish and incense.

Lungs of the world!

Do you know that forests are called 'the lungs of the world'? But why are they called that? Because the many trees in forests take in carbon-dioxide and give out oxygen, helping to generate more breathing air for animals and humans. That's the reason we should not cut down all the trees, but instead we should plant as many trees as possible. Trees also help in controlling global warming, so 'go green'!

FLOWERS

Fragrance or smell?

We all know that Rafflesia is the largest flower. Some species of this five-petalled flower, such as the Rafflesia arnoldi, can be as big as 39 inches and as heavy as 10 kilograms! But do you know that the Rafflesia flower has another 'quality' about it? Well, it is an extremely smelly flower. It smells like rotting flesh and is called the corpse flower (a name that it shared with the Titan Arum plant).

Family ties!

Bamboo plants have some amazing traits. They are strange in the way they grow in a day's time – some up to a couple of feet! But what is more interesting is their flowering habit. There are many varieties of the bamboo plant with different flowering cycles. What is special is that the ones of each species will flower exactly at the same time – no matter where they are! Family ties?

Titan!

Don't judge the Titan Arum only by what you have just read. It is the smelliest flower, yes; but it is also credited with the tallest bloom. An example of this was grown by Louis Ricciardiello of the USA. And how tall did it grow? Well, 10 ft 2.25 in. It was on display at Winnipesaukee Orchids in Gilford, New Hampshire when this height was calculated. Imagine, the smell grows too with the flower!

Too old for a flower!

Most plants that we have seen grow flowers almost every year but not all. There are some plants that take much longer. For example, the century plant, or agave, takes years to grow one flower and then it dies! And stranger still is a rare plant called Puya raimondii which takes 150 years to grow a flower and then dies! So much for a bunch of flowers!

Noble white!

Where does the edelweiss get its name from? From two German words – 'edel' meaning noble and 'weiss' meaning white, together making 'noble whiteness'. Did you know that this noble white plant is very protective about the way it looks? The edelweiss flower has hairs which protect it from the Sun and winds. Protection therapy!

Colour changer!

The Giant Amazon Water Lily has a very interesting pollination system! The flower before pollination is white in colour and in the evenings, it smells like a pineapple which attracts the pollinator beetle. At this point, the flower is female and receptive to pollen. When the day starts, the flower closes with the beetle inside. During the day, the flower changes to male, coating the beetle with pollen. The flower opens again in the evening but the colour changes to pink by then which the beetle doesn't like and moves on to another white flower to pollinate it!

RECORD HOLDERS

Old is gold!

The oldest tree to be planted by a human (and not natural seeding) is 2300 years old! It is a sacred fig tree called Sri Maha Bodhiya in Anuradhapura, Sri Lanka. Do you know what is so special about the tree in addition to the fact that it is the oldest tree planted by a human? The mother tree of this specimen is none other than the famous Bodhi Tree under which Gautam Buddha gained enlightenment. Enlightening, isn't it?

Older than the oldest!

That was about the oldest tree. Now it's time for the oldest surviving species. The oldest surviving species of trees is the Maidenhair (Ginkgo biloba) of Zhejiang, China. Scientists have estimated that the first of the kind would have existed around 160 million years ago! I am sure it would be difficult for the trees to make their 'family tree'!

Another category!

Between the two you have just read about, there is another category that needs a special mention. Why does it need a special mention? Because that tree is special when compared to many Cypress trees you may have seen. The special Cypress is the Sarv-e-Abarkooh, or Zoroastrian Sarv. This tree is 4,000 years old and has been declared a national monument in Iran.

Number game!

Do you know what chromosomes do? Well, they contain all the genetic information about an organism. Every living being has chromosomes; we humans have 46 chromosomes in 23 pairs. Other organisms have either more or less. But the adder's tongue fern beats all the organisms – it has 1,440 chromosomes arranged in 720 pairs. That's not only the highest in plants but in all organisms!

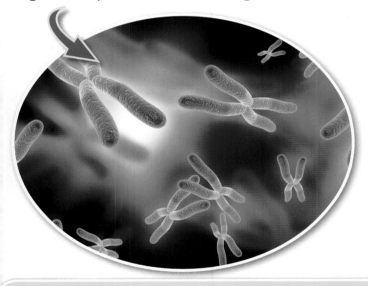

That's a tall one!

Redwoods are the tallest trees in the world. They grow up to a height of hundreds of feet. And the tallest of the lot is the Hyperion. At 379.1 feet, this tree is a giant! And if you want to meet this giant, you will have to go to Redwood National Park, California, USA.

Deadly plant!

Do you know that there is a plant which is deadlier than the venom of a rattlesnake? And not just a little but 12,000 times more toxic than the venom? Castor bean has the distinction of being the most toxic common plant. Ricin – the toxin found in castor seeds is 6000 times more toxic than cyanide! It causes the clumping and breakdown of red blood cells which leads to internal bleeding.

How are mountains formed?

How do you think mountains form? Well, it's not a day's or a year's work but it takes millions of years for a mountain to form. Though there are various ways in which mountains can be created, most of the Earth's major mountains are a result of tectonic movements below the surface of the Earth. The tectonic plates move and bang against each other causing a part of the plates to buckle. Over millions of years of plate movements and buckling, mountains are created.

Taller than the tallest!

Mauna Kea, a volcano on the island of Hawaii in the US, is the world's tallest mountain. From the base to the peak, it measures 10,205 metres. Then why is Mount Everest considered the tallest mountain? Because 6000 metres of Mauna Kea is under water! Only 4.205 metres is above sea level and that height is half of Mount Everest's 8850 metres!

What's in a range?

What is a mountain range? A mountain range is a continuous chain of mountains. Now that you know what is a mountain range, do you know which is the longest mountain range of the world? It is the Andes in South America. Over 7000 kilometres long, the Andes is home to many high volcanoes including Ojos del Salado, the world's highest volcano on the Chile/Argentina border.

I am growing!

Mountains keep growing. Every year when researchers take their measurements, they realise that the mountains are higher by a millimetre or two. The mountain growing at the most amazing speed is the Nanga Parbat in Pakistan which is growing at a rate of 7 millimetres every year. It is estimated that this mountain started developing 30–50 million years ago – and it is still growing, not bad at all!

Strange!

Did you know that Antarctica is a mountainous terrain, unlike the flat ground that we had thought it was? This was discovered when some mysterious peaks started appearing here and there. Researchers got to work almost immediately and what they found out was startling. Antarctica is a mountain range that formed millions of years ago. Eventually it started getting covered in ice until ice filled all the troughs, settled there and made a thick flat surface!

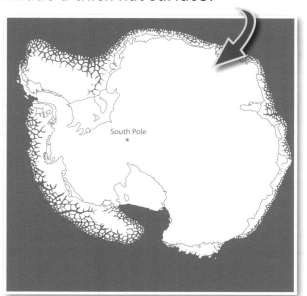

South Pole

The Mount!

Mount Everest is the tallest mountain in the world measuring a record 8850 metres above sea level. It is known as Sagarmatha in Nepal and Chomolungma in China (it separates the two countries). It is common knowledge that the first people to climb the Everest were Hillary and Tenzing but one school of thought is that Sir George Mallory had reached its summit first. Since he died on his way back, it is difficult to say whether he did or not. The truth with Mallory is buried high up in the snow.

LOWS

Safe to the deepest!

What's a cave? It is a hollow opening in the ground, a horizontal opening in a hill or a mountain. Caves can be very deep sometimes. The deepest of all was discovered in 2007 by a group of cavers who reached a record depth of 2,191 metres in the Krubera Cave (it is also called the Voronya Cave) in the Arabika Masiff in Georgia.

Underwater caving?

An underwater cave system?!
Sistema Ox Bel Ha, which means 'three paths in water' in the Mayan language, is the longest underground cave system in Quintana Roo, one of three states forming Mexico's Yucatan Peninsula. Ox Bel Ha is a series of complicated underwater caves and is a classic example of coastal caves. These caves have been made accessible by lakes called cenotes. Many kilometres of the longest underground cave have been explored and cavers believe that they have still many more kilometres to go!

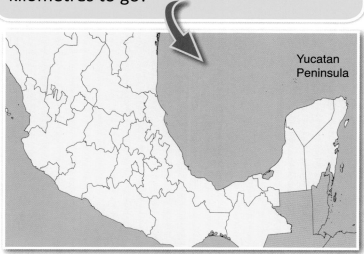

Yucatan Peninsula

Deadly low!

From where do we measure the height of the mountains or the depths of sea? From sea level. And what is sea level? Sea level is the average height of the sea measured at a point which is midway between high tides and low tides. Calculating from sea level, the lowest exposed ground is the shore of the Dead Sea in Israel/Jordon. It goes without saying that the sea bed is even lower, by almost 728 metres.

Deepest valley!

The deepest valley is found at 'the roof of the world' which has an average altitude of 4,900 metres and the highest altitude of 8850 metres! Yes, you guessed right, the deepest valley is in Tibet. The Yarlung Zangbo valley between the Namche Barwa peak on one side and Jala Peri on the other, has an average depth of 5000 metres but the deepest point is 5,382 metres deep – this is three times the depth of the Grand Canyon! That sure is very deep, isn't it?

The grandeur of the canyon!

The Grand Canyon is the largest land gorge in the world, and no one created it. It's in fact nature's gift to mankind – the process started almost six million years ago when the Colorado river started eroding the river bed. It is 1.6 kilometres deep and the width varies from 0.5–29 kilometres. The Grand Canyon contains several major ecosystems; and an incredible four million people visit this wonderful site every year.

The joys of a deep mine!

Tau Tona (it means the great lion) is the deepest mine in the world. Situated in Carletonville in South Africa, it is literally a gold mine! Mining here started in 1962 and in 2008, the miners had managed to mine down to 3.9 kilometres. The gold mine now has 800 kilometres of tunnels and around 5,600 miners earn their living by working in this mine.

LAND AND WATER

Boiling hot!

What are geysers? Geysers are jets of hot water and steam which erupt from the ground. Now you must be wondering how the water gets heated beneath the ground? The answer is volcanic activity. The Yellowstone National Park in the US has the largest number of geysers – there are 500 active geysers there, the most famous being the Old Faithful, which erupts every 91 minutes.

Amazing Amazon!

The volume of water that flows from the mouth of a river to the basin depends on the season. For example, in hot and dry seasons it reduces; and in monsoons it increases. The largest river in the world is the great Amazon. It discharges around 200,000 m^3/sec of water into the Atlantic Ocean! And when the river is flooding, the quantity goes up to 340,000 m^3/sec. Water, water everywhere!

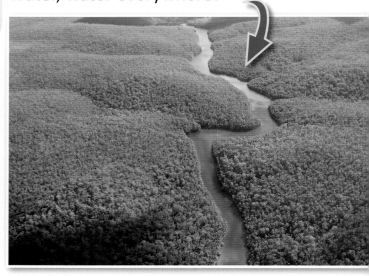

Freezing!

Do you know how glaciers are formed? Large areas of snow and ice that reach their point of ablation after centuries make glaciers. You can describe glaciers as frozen rivers of ice which move very slowly. Glaciers can be any size. The longest glacier is Lambert-Fischer glacier in Antarctica which was discovered only in 1956! Glaciers cover 10 per cent of the Earth. How much water is that? Well, if all the glaciers of the world melted, the sea level would rise by 70 metres! That is how much water they contain!

Warming up!

Oceans are huge areas of saline water which cover over 70 percent of the Earth's surface. The Pacific Ocean is the largest ocean, followed by the Atlantic Ocean and then the Indian Ocean. Did you know that the Indian Ocean, which accounts for 20 percent out of 70 percent total for oceans, has the warmest surface temperature of all the oceans? Why?

Well, because most of it is in the tropics.

Falling stories!

Waterfalls form when a river or a stream drops from a higher level to a lower level. These are created in the river's youth due to erosion. Waterfalls can be of 12 different types – block, cascade, cataract, chute, fan, frozen, horsetail, plunge, punchbowl, segmented, tiered, and multi-stepped. The tallest waterfall is Angel Falls with a total drop of 979 metres. But the largest falls by vertical area is Victoria Falls. This covers an area of 184,400 square metres.

Break off!

When a piece of land breaks off from a larger piece of land or continent and gets surrounded by water on all sides, an island is born. Greenland is the largest island in the world. So large that the equivalent of three Texas states can fit inside Greenland. Did you know that Madagascar in the Indian Ocean is the oldest island in the world? It broke off from the main Indian subcontinent almost 80–100 million years ago!

The first ones!

Before we start talking about the ancient civilizations, we must know who were the first to claim the title of 'ancient civilizations'. These were the Mesopotamian civilization, Egyptian civilization, Indus Valley Civilization and the Chinese civilization. Although these civilizations were thousands of kilometres away from one another, they had a few things in common – all of them built cities, invented forms of writing to communicate and record, made pottery, used metals, domesticated animals developed a social system and worked around the city.

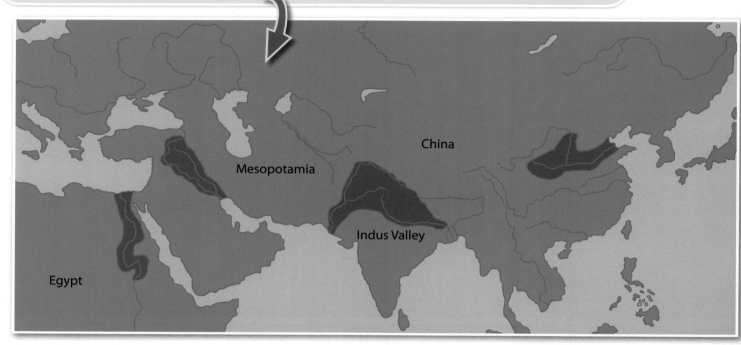

Gearing up!

The Egyptians used to embalm their dead and then mummify them. This is a known fact. What is less well known is the fact that around that time, other civilizations were also mummifying their dead. More than 1000 mummies have been found in Xinjiang, China. In fact, the oldest-known mummy was found in Chile and was from 5050 B.C.! All these civilizations had a similar way of embalming, just like their Egyptian friends.

New home!

How did the pyramids come into being? It was the duty of the prime minister to construct the king's tomb. When the king was put to rest, great structures were built which are now known as pyramids. To help the king survive in the afterlife, food and other objects of utility were kept in the tomb. And images of pet animals were painted on the tomb walls, thinking that they would protect the dead. In some cases, pets, such as cats, and servants were also buried along with the king!

Superpowers!

The Egyptians were very religious. How else can you justify more than 2000 gods! But out of the 2000, nine made it into the Great Ennead (nine major gods and goddesses) – Atum, Shu, Tefnut, Geb, Nut, Osiris, Isis, Set, and Nephthys. Horus, the falcon-headed God, was introduced to the Ennead and is said to be the son of Isis and Osiris. The two main centres of religion in ancient Egypt were Heliopolis and Memphis.

Horus!

Horus wasn't originally one of the Ennead. He was considered the sky god and patron of the king. Born to Isis, after Set murdered his father, Osiris, Horus was raised to avenge his father's death. He fought with Set for 80 years till the gods finally relented and gave him the throne of Egypt. Horus was an epitome of excellence and every Egyptian king was considered a living form of Horus. Horus is also depicted as a hawk-headed man.

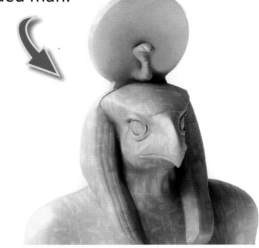

Amun or Amun Ra?

Amun, whose name means the Invincible One, was the ancient Egyptian god of air. Amun was adopted to the Ennead of Heliopolis when he merged with the Sun God Ra, thus becoming Amun Ra. So, whether you call him Amun or Amun Ra, you are talking about the same one. Though he is generally depicted as a man wearing two plumes on his head, with a sceptre in his hand, he has always been associated with a number of animals – goose, snake, ram, frog, crocodile, ape and many more super animals like the one where he has a body of a beetle, the wings of a hawk, the legs of a man and the paws and claws of a lion!

Indeed Indus!

When compared to the other civilizations of the time, the Indus Valley Civilization was the greatest of them all. It was one of the world's earliest urban societies. The greatness of the civilization that existed 5000 years ago can be summed up from the fact that they 'designed' their cities, had highly developed architecture, their ornaments and arts are still unparalleled, and their management of economy and trade is a marvel. Facts about the civilization would be clearer had the Indus script been already deciphered. But it looks like it would be a few more years before it is deciphered and we finally have more understanding of the ancient Indus people.

The big one!

The Indus Valley Civilization had many cities – Harappa, Mohen-jodaro, Dholavira, Kalibangan, Rakhigarhi, Ganeriwala, Rupal and Lothal. But the most important and largest of them was the city of Harappa. Archaeologists have managed to uncover an entire section which has helped them to understand the civilization better. The other important city is Mohen-jodaro. Brick work in Mohen-jodaro is a masterpiece. They tell the history of the city through the construction of drains and wells, gullies and walls.

Who were the Hellenes?

The Ancient Greeks called themselves 'Hellenes' and their land 'Hella'. They named it after the legendary hero Hellen. You must be wondering why it is called Greece then? That is because when the Romans came, they gave Greece this name, and it stuck. Ancient Greeks, or Hellenes, had a very structured system. Men were supposed to handle public matters, while matters of home were left to women. Slavery was such an important part of their life that for them only two kinds of people existed in their little world – free people and slaves.

Planning!

It would be unfair to say that only Mohen-jodaro had amazing brick work. Even Harappa and Dholavira used same-sized bricks and standardised weights. The best thing about these cities was the fact that they were planned. Most of our new cities are not planned, but people many thousands of years ago had the focus and determination to do something quite difficult, especially then. Streets were wide, sewage systems were in place, public and private wells were present in large numbers, and people were provided with reservoirs and bathing platforms. It is difficult to find such planned and organised cities in nowadays, so imagine how difficult would it have been when the Indus people did it?

Time for festivities!

Ancient Greeks believed in a pantheon of Gods and in order to keep them happy, they would celebrate festivals. What is interesting is the fact that the festivals had competitions, which were considered a way to honour the gods. People would compete in different fields – poetry, music, theatre and even athletics. The athletic competitions gave birth to the Olympic Games which were played in honour of Zeus. It is believed that the first Olympic Games were played in 776 B.C.!

The birthplace!

Ancient Greece is called the birthplace of the western civilization. The ancient Greeks showed the world a new way of life – and the Greek city states became centres of arts, learning and politics. Great philosophers like Aristotle, Socrates and Aristophanes were Greeks. Talking about these great learned men, do you know that the word alphabet comes from the first two letters of the Greek alphabet – alpha and beta?

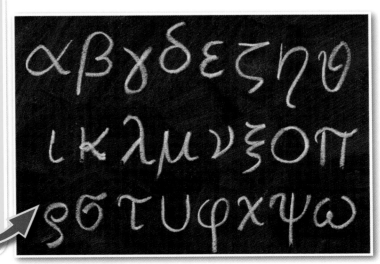

Meso Meso!

Present-day Turkey, Syria and Iraq made up the ancient Mesopotamian region. Mesopotamia lay comfortably between two great rivers — Tigris and Euphrates. Mesopotamia was controlled by many different peoples at different times. The Sumerians reached Mesopotamia in the 4th century B.C. And do you know they introduced the world to — the wheel and the cuneiform script.
They are said to have invented both!

Mathematicians!

The Mayas were extremely talented people who built amazing temples which showed an understanding of mathematics. The temple of Kukulcan (dedicated to a god similar to God Quetzalcoatl in whom the Aztecs believed) in Chichen Itza is a 98 ft high step pyramid. It has been made so accurately that on the spring and autumn equinoxes, the northwest corner of the pyramid casts a series of triangular shadows which look like a wriggling snake. It is believed that it was intentionally done for their god Kukulcan who is a feathered-serpent god!

Most ancient!

People have been known to live in China since 1600 B.C. making it one of the first places to support civilization. Initially, people were divided in small kingdoms, but by 221 B.C. all of them united under one emperor. The ancient Chinese were far ahead of their time and also of any other civilization. They were great inventors – the paper you write on was invented by them, the gunpowder that is used in the crackers that you pull was invented by them, the matches that you use to light candles were invented by them, the compass that you use to find directions was invented by them, the umbrella that you use to protect yourself from rain was invented by them. They also invented a seismograph to measure earthquakes; and many more things!

How Rome came into being

Rome was the centre of the ancient Roman Empire. There is a very interesting story about the origin of Rome. The story is about two brothers Romulus and Remus, who were the sons of Mars, the Roman god of war. When they were still babies, the boys were kidnapped and thrown into the River Tiber. They were rescued by a she-wolf who fed them as one of her own. When they grew up, they met Mars who asked them to build a city on the site they were raised. And that is how Rome was built. This is probably the most famous legend in world history.

The Mayas and their predictions

The Mayan Empire stretched across southern Mexico and northern central America. They were specialists of time and made 17 calendars for different purposes! The precision with which these complex calendars were built, demonstrates the intelligence of these people who lived thousands of years ago. Many believe that the Mayan calendar ends on 21st December 2012 suggesting that the world will end then. Whether is a myth or it reality, only time will tell.

ANCIENT WORLD

Alexander the Great!

Alexander III of Macedonia, also known as Alexander the Great, was probably the greatest emperor of the ancient world. He lived only for 33 years (he was born in 356 B.C. and died in 323 B.C.) but what he achieved in those 33 years was exemplary. He built an empire that covered modern Iraq, Iran, Syria and Turkey. After his death, none of his generals had the charisma or strength to hold his empire together and it collapsed soon after.

The undecipherable!

We know a lot about the Indus Valley Civilization but we haven't managed to decipher their text. Why? That is because their text is very brief and short. Text on seals have an average of 5 symbols, some others have more but they are exceptions. Plus, there is no other language that is even vaguely similar to that of the Indus Valley. How much more will we understand and know of the great civilization when their script is finally deciphered? These are the mysteries of the ancient world!

All for love!

King Nebuchadnezzar loved his wife so much that he made a garden for her – a garden that had exotic plants imported from all over the world. The garden also had animals and rare species. The fact that King Nebuchadnezzar was ruling a large part of the world helped him assemble plants and animals from any place in his kingdom. We are talking about the Hanging Gardens of Babylon. It was so beautiful that it is considered one of the seven wonders of the ancient world.

Lost and found!

In the early 20th century, archaeologist Arthur Evans discovered a civilization which flourished in the Bronze age between 27th and 15th century B.C. on the island of Crete. He named it 'Minoan' after King Minos. Why? Because King Minos, a mythical Greek ruler who is believed to have ruled Crete, is renowned for having kept the Minotaur in a complex labyrinth and Evans found a similar labyrinth-like structure on one of the sites.

Homer and his works

That's not all for the ancient world. It was around the 8th century B.C. that there lived the ancient greek epic poet Homer. He is credited with being one of the great poets – not only in his time but of all time. Homer penned the Iliad and the Odyssey, two epics, which talk about the lives and times of ancient Greece's two most famous warriors – Achilles and Odysseus. Translations of these books are available in many languages and they form part of many curricula as well.

Colossal Colossus!

The Colossus of Rhodes was another marvel of the ancient world. It was a 107 ft tall statue of the greek titan Helios which was constructed between 292 and 280 B.C. on the island of Rhodes in Greece. The statue was destroyed during an earthquake that hit the island in 226 B.C. But then why wasn't it rebuilt? Because the oracle at Delphi said that the statue fell because the people had offended Helios. In fear of his wrath, the statue was never rebuilt.

MEDIEVAL WORLD

Middle Ages!

The Middle Age is a period that lasted from 500 AD to 1500 AD. The Middle Ages witnessed the life of one of the greatest rulers in history – Charlemagne. Also known as Charles the Great, Charlemagne built an empire which covered most parts of present-day France and Germany. His conquests were so great that he was crowned emperor in 800 AD. And the day was the most celebration-filled day of the year – Christmas. But Charlemagne was the emperor for a period of only fourteen years as he died on 28th January 814. Before his death, he crowned his son Louis the Pious as the new emperor.

Aztec Rule!

The Aztecs arrived in Mexico in the 14th century and founded the city of Tenochtitlan. They were nomadic people who had great knowledge of engineering and architecture. But at heart, they were warriors. They extended their empire from the Pacific to the Gulf of Mexico and Guatemala! It is said that they were masters of weaponry, and some of their weapons were so sharp that they could bring down the head of a horse in one blow!

Coming of the Incas!

The medieval world saw the coming of the Incas. The Inca Empire was the largest empire in pre-Columbian America. It stretched 900,000 square kilometres and covered Columbia, Bolivia and Argentina. The capital city was Cuzco in modern-day Peru. The Incas were very organised people and led a well-structured life. They had a governing body. The commoners would work for themselves and the governing body and in return the governing body would take care of their needs. The Inca Civilization did not have a very long life though. It started off in the 13th century and was crushed by the Spanish invaders in the 16th century.

Knights in shining armour!

The Middle Ages is a very interesting period in the British history and is full of stories of knights. To become a night, a person needed to be trained as a page for seven years and then a squire for another seven. Only then could he become a knight. Did you know that the word squire comes from a French word esquire? Not surprisingly, esquire means shield bearer. It is interesting to know that knights wore scarves, veils or sleeves – a lady's 'favours' – while jousting!

What an invention!

Talking about knights, it wouldn't have been possible for them to fight on horseback if it had not been for this invention. It allowed the knights to manoeuvre their horses easily and even carry more weapons. And what was the invention? The stirrup! It is believed that the stirrup was first made in India and was being used there for a long time before it reached Europe in 700's.

Black Death!

The Middle Ages witnessed the most devastating epidemic in history – the Black Death! It was an outbreak of bubonic plague which spread to all parts of the world via the trade routes! It peaked in England between 1348 and 1350 and killed almost one-third of the population. The plague would cause swellings in the skin and blackening around areas. And when blood was let out from that area, it was found to be greenish black! Hence the name 'Black Death'.

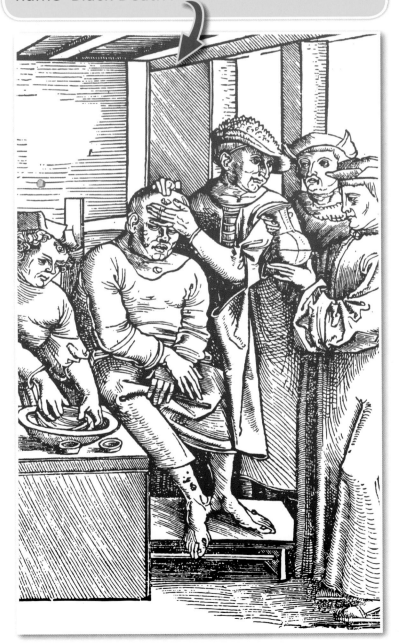

MODERN WORLD

Long live the king!

Modern history talks about two monarchs who have been credited with ruling for the longest time. One is King Louis XIV of France who is the longest-reigning world monarch. He ruled from 1643 to 1715 – a period of 72 years! The second is Queen Victoria of Britain. She is the longest reigning British monarch. She took the crown a little after her 18th birthday in 1837 and ruled until she was 81 – a total of 63.5 years.

Organisations!

Modern history has also witnessed the creation of some of the world's most important organisations. The most important of them being the United Nations, which was founded in 1945 to take decisions about peace-keeping and human rights; followed by United Nations Educational, Scientific and Cultural Organisation (UNESCO) in 1946; and United Nations Children's Fund (UNICEF) in 1947. The World Bank, World Trade Organisation, World Health Organisation, NATO and many more were also founded in the 20th century.

Four seasons and four freedoms!

You know about the four seasons, don't you? But do you know about the four freedoms? 'Four freedoms' made an essential part of a very famous speech by President Roosevelt, a speech that he delivered on 6th January 1941 during World War II. In this speech, Roosevelt said that four freedoms – freedom of speech, freedom of worship, freedom from want and freedom from fear – were very important for any democracy. The four-fold path of Roosevelt.

The great sinking!

The sinking of the Titanic was probably one of the saddest events of modern history. RMS Titanic was constructed at the Harland

and Wolff shipyard in Belfast, Ireland. It set sail on 10th April 1912 from Southampton and was bound for New York with 2200 people on board. On its maiden voyage, the Titanic was the largest vessel afloat. Four days into the journey, the Titanic collided with an iceberg and sunk killing 1500 people. Did you know that the Titanic was engineered to be an 'unsinkable' ship!

The partition and independence!

One of the most famous events of modern history is the partition and independence of India. India had been a colony of the British Empire and at that time a quarter of the people in the world lived under British rule. After years of struggle for freedom, India and Pakistan were made two states and given independence in August 1947.

Inventions galore!

20th century onwards the world has seen a boom of inventions – aeroplane, car, television, telephone, vacuum cleaner, razor, mobile phone, computer, tablets – almost everything was invented in the 20th century!

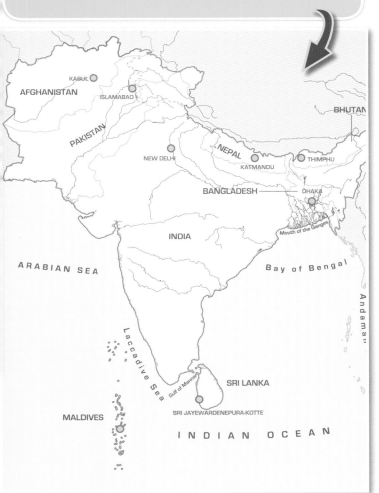

ASIA

Where does it belong?

Do you know the name of the only city that falls in two continents? It is partly in Asia and partly in Europe? Did you get the name? Long ago, in ancient times, it was first known as Byzantium and then as Constantinople. The answer is Istanbul!

Istanbul is in Turkey which is considered a part of Asia because a large part of the country is in Asia. The territory west of the Bosphorus Strait is in Europe.

Great wall!

The Great Wall of China doesn't need a long introduction, does it? It is an 8,851 kilometre long wall, the construction for which started as long ago as the 5th century B.C. to protect the country from nomadic invaders. Many rulers added to the wall, the most recent addition was made in the 16th century. The Great Wall is a combination of walls, trenches, hills and rivers!

Biggest!

Still on the subject of China, here is another point that needs a mention – China has the biggest population in the world, with India not very far behind! The reason for this is simple – more people are born every day than die. Therefore, China has enforced a one-child-per-family limit. As a result, China's population is stabilising whereas India's population is still increasing.

The largest!

The largest country in the world stretches from Europe to Asia. Russia with a total area of 16,888,500 square kilometres is the largest country in the world. It is so large that it covers 13 per cent of the world's land area! Russia was one of the main republics of the Union of Soviet Socialist Republics (USSR). Russia voluntarily accepted all Soviet foreign debt and claimed overseas Soviet properties as its own.

Greatness!

One of the most important and easily recognisable structures of the Indus Valley Civilization is the Great Bath. You would not find ostentatious temples, palaces or houses in the Indus Valley civilization but you would find places like the public bath. It is believed that the Great Bath was used for performing religious or spiritual rights. The Great Bath had a layer of tar to prevent any leakage and the drainage was designed in such a way that dirty water was routed to the drains connected to the streets. And since these baths were water-tight compartments, there was no chance of this dirty water getting back in.

Peace for all!

The man who changed the way the world fought! He fought for his rights but in the most peaceful and non-violent way! The man is none other than Mohandas Karamchand Gandhi, also known as Mahatma Gandhi or the Mahatma. Indians lovingly call him 'Bapu', Hindi for father (he is the father of the nation in India). A lawyer by profession, Gandhi negotiated with the British for years until they left in 1947. Gandhi's non-violent struggle for freedom was so exemplary that he found followers in great people like Martin Luther King Junior and Nelson Mandela.

The fighter!

Nelson Mandela is synonymous with will power and determination. He spent many years of his life in prison — not for any wrong that he had committed but because he wanted to give the people of his country what was rightfully due to them — freedom from apartheid! He was arrested in 1964 at the age of 46, and when he was released in 1990, he was an old man! But he won the battle in the end. In 1994, he was elected the President of South Africa in the first fully democratic election held in the country. And for all that he did for his country, he was awarded the Nobel Peace Prize in 1993.

Egypt!

Egypt is very strategically located in north Africa as it has a coastline on the Mediterranean Sea as well as the Red Sea. Now you know why one of the most important ancient civilizations thrived on this fertile piece of land. Egypt shares its border with Sudan, Libya, Israel and the Gaza Strip and controls the Suez Canal. Therefore, trade is simple. Egypt is also considered one of the leading military powers of the Middle East.

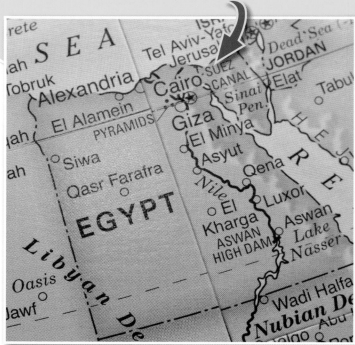

Wildlife!

Africa is also known for its wildlife. It is home to the hippopotamus, lion, crocodile, white rhinoceros, black mamba, gazelle, great white shark, buffalo, African elephant, puff adder, and many more. Did you know that the rhinoceros and many more are now endangered species!

Longest of all!

Africa is home to the longest river in the world – the Nile. 6695 kilometres long, the Nile flows through Kenya, Eritrea, Congo, Burundi, Uganda, Tanzania, Rwanda, Egypt, Sudan and Ethiopia. It is in the Nile delta that the Rosetta stone was found – the stone that is considered to be the key to Ancient Egypt and Ancient Egyptians.

Some more...

Egypt is the most visited country in Africa. Africa is also home to 3000 ethnic groups who use around 2000 languages to communicate, Arabic being the most widely used. It is estimated that over 170 million people talk in Arabic.

The Great Rift Valley

All the continents at some point of time were part of Africa and eventually broke up into smaller continents. Geologists are saying that there is going to be another new continent sooner or later. Africa is being split into two! Also known as the East African Rift, the Great Rift Valley extends southwards from the Afar Triple Junction. Geologists believe that eventually this rift will split the African plate into two different plates – the Nubian Plate and the Somali Plate.

AUSTRALIA

Longest reef!

The Great Barrier Reef in Australia is the longest reef in the world. It is 2,027 kilometres long! Did you know that it is not one giant structure but many small structures that have grown together? In fact, the Great Barrier Reef is also the largest marine structure built by living creatures – it is home to billions of dead and living corals!

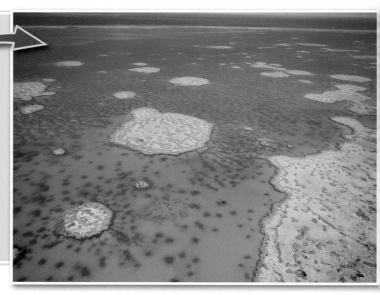

Original or aboriginal!

Aboriginal is a term that is used to describe the 'original' people of Australia – people who have been living there for thousands of years. It is believed that aborigines lived in Africa (back then, everybody lived in Africa!) and they started walking towards Australia 70,000 years ago. Almost 20,000 years later they reached Australia! It is thought that a land 'bridge' connected Eurasia and Australia thousands of years ago and that is how they managed to walk to Australia – which is now an island!

A rock or a mountain?

Ayers rock is the largest freestanding rock in the world. You must be wondering how big a rock can be? Well, this one is 3.6 kilometres long, 2 kilometres wide and 335 metres high! Amazing isn't it?! Located in the northern territory in Australia, Ayers Rock is locally known as 'Uluru', the name given it by the local aborigines for whom the rock is sacred.

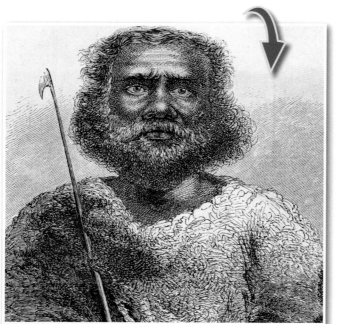

I recognise!

Sydney has some of the most recognisable and important structures in Australia. The Opera House took 11 years and $102 million to build! Sydney's harbour is the deepest natural harbour in the world and the Sydney Harbour Bridge is the widest long-span bridge in the world. Plenty feathers in the cap!

Desert!

Australia is the driest continent in the world and has the second largest desert of the world, the Australian desert – which includes the Gibson, Great Victorian, Great Sandy and Simpson deserts – is in Australia (the world's largest is the Sahara desert in Africa). The Devil's Marbles, two rocks balanced against each other, can be seen in the Australian Desert and are sacred to the aborigines.

Unique!

Australia is home to many animals, some of them quite unique. In fact, many of them can't be found anywhere else. Can you name some? The kangaroo, the largest living marsupial, is found only in Australia. Also the dingo (a wild form of domestic dog), kookaburra (a bird), platypus (a monotreme), dugong (an aquatic animal), Tasmanian devil (largest carnivorous marsupial) and the koala (another marsupial) are all special to Australia.

EUROPE

Who gave the name?

Where does Europe get its name from? It is believed that Europe is named after Princess Europa, a beautiful Phoenician princess in Greek mythology. Legend has it that Princess Europa was so beautiful that when Zeus saw her, he fell in love with her almost immediately, and that he took the form of a bull to abduct her!

The lost cities!

Two Italian cities were lost for around 1700 years. A volcanic eruption from Mount Vesuvius, which lasted two days, buried the cities of Pompeii and Herculaneum under ash and pumice in A.D. 79. The city was accidently discovered in 1748. Many years and many excavations later we now know what a wonderful city Pompeii once was. Many treasures have been discovered along with well-preserved murals! Many people were buried alive and have been found in the same position as they were when covered by ash!

Smallest and largest!

Europe is the second smallest continent in the world. And it houses the smallest country in the world – the Vatican City - which is spread over an area of around 100 acres and has around 900 residents. That's the smallest. Now, a bit about the largest country. Did you know that Russia, the largest country in the world, is in Asia as well as Europe? The part west of the Ural Mountains is in Europe and is known as European Asia. Its biggest cities such as St. Petersburg and Moscow are in Europe.

Ferris wheel!

Known as the Millennium Wheel, or more popularly as the London Eye, this giant Ferris wheel was the largest in the world till it was surpassed by the Star of Nanchang (in 2006) and then the Singapore Flyer (in 2008). Situated on the bank of river Thames in London, the London Eye has an average 3.5 million customers every year. Did you know it can carry 800 people per revolution? Considering its size and the view, you wouldn't be surprised that is it named the London Eye!

No cars!

Venice has always been known as the floating city because of the bridges and canals, but do you know how that happened? There were 118 submerged islands in the northern end of the Adriatic Sea. Wood pilings were set in and the parts of the city were connected by 400 foot bridges and 170 boat canals.

The beautiful Alps!

Stunningly beautiful Alps run from France to Austria and Slovenia. The most famous peaks in the Alps are the Matterhorn and Mont Blanc. The Swiss Alps, which are one part of the Alps, are home to the longest rail tunnel in the world - the Gotthard train tunnel. The 57 kilometre long tunnel will open to the public in 2016.

Finding gold!

What would happen if someone came to your classroom and said there's gold in the playground? Everyone would run to the playground, right? That's what happened when James Marshall found gold in California - people from all over the world travelled there. Some became very rich and some went back home with a little more than what they had started with. This rush for gold is called the California Gold Rush and lasted from 1848 to 1855.

The Island State of USA

Do you know the name of the newest state in The US? The newest state is Hawaii (recognised as a state on 21st August 1959). Hawaii is the only state in the US that is made up entirely of islands – eight of them. The volcanic activity in Hawaii has made it a very important tourist spot. In fact, the world's most active volcano, Kilauea, has been erupting on a continuous basis since 1983 and is in Hawaii.

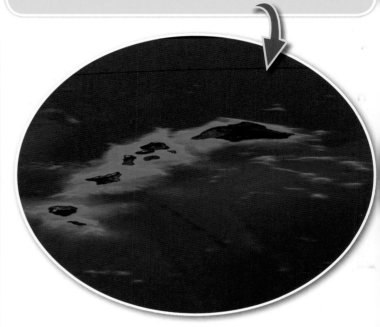

Five siblings!

Did you know that there is a group of five lakes on the USA-Canada border? Called the 'great lakes', they are Lake Superior, Lake Huron, Lake Michigan, Lake Erie and Lake Ontario. Lake Superior is so called because it is higher upstream than the other four.

Aha B-aha-ma!

Do you know where Columbus landed first when he set sail aboard the Santa Maria, the Pinta and the Nina for India? Not in India but in the Bahamas, he found America instead! The Bahamas has 700 islands but only 30 are inhabited. And do you know how popular it is? So much so, that an estimated four million tourists visit the Bahamas every year!

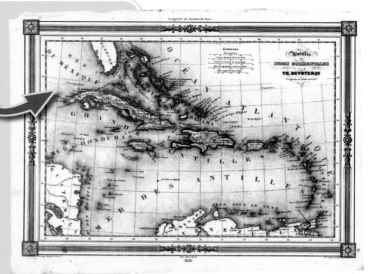

Officially yours!

Do you know the official name of Mexico? It is known as the United Mexican States. The Mexican flag has three stripes – green stands for hope, white stands for purity, and red represents the blood of the Mexican people. The most interesting part is the Eagle – the Aztecs, who were nomads, settled in Mexico because they saw an eagle (which represents the Sun) perched on a cactus (which represents the heart) clutching a snake (which represents the earth or God Quetzalcoatl). The same scene can now be seen on the flag.

Longest coastline!

Which country in North America has the longest coastline in the world? Hint: If you 'Can' think of the first three letters, you will get the name! The answer is Canada! It has a total coastline of approximately 265,523 kilometres! And it also has more inland lakes and rivers than any other country in the world.

SOUTH AMERICA

Instant skeletons!

What fish will you find in South America? Piranha! Piranha are fish of the Amazon basin which are capable of ripping flesh from an animal in less than a minute leaving only the skeleton behind. Piranha are small, but are smart – they stay in packs of hundreds and are armed with small, razor-like teeth. Out of more than 25 species of piranha, the red belly piranha is the most fearsome. How did the piranha get their fearsome reputation? The locals put on a display for the then President of the US, Theodore Roosevelt, during which a cow was thrown to starving piranha and they devoured it to the bone in matter of minutes.

lungs of our planet. Did you know that one fourth of all our medicines are derived from only 1% of the tropical rainforests which have been tested by scientists? Imagine how much more is left to find!

The driest place!

Welcome to the Atacama desert – it is the driest place on Earth and runs along a 1000 kilometre stretch on the coast of Chile up to the border of Peru. There is even a part of the desert where the soil looks similar to that found on Mars. That's the reason why many movies and television series such as 'Space Odyssey: Voyage To The Planets' have shot their Mars scenes in the Atacama Desert.

Ama-zing-zon!

The Amazon Rainforest (Amazonia) constitutes half of the Earth's tropical rainforest and is said to contain one in every ten known species on the planet. The forests of Amazonia recycle carbon dioxide and release one fifth of the planet's oxygen – so now you know why the Amazon Rainforests are called the

The oldies!

South America also finds Machu Picchu, a symbol of the Incan Empire. Built around 1450, Machu Picchu is a World Heritage Site and a Modern Wonder. Set 7000 feet above sea level in the Andes Mountains, Machu Picchu has around 150 buildings

including a bath, houses, temples and sanctuaries. Luckily it was so isolated, or like many other sites, this too would have been destroyed by the Spanish invaders.

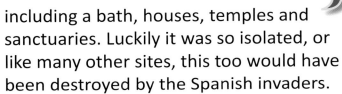

Record holder Continent!

South America is the fourth largest continent in the world – it covers an area of approximately 17,849,000 square kilometres. It is politically divided into twelve sovereign states – Argentina, Bolivia, Brazil, Chile, Colombia, Ecuador, Guyana, Paraguay, Peru, Suriname, Uruguay and Venezuela, and the overseas administration of French Guiana. South America boasts some of the world's extremes – the largest river (Amazon), the largest rainforest (Amazonian Rainforest), the largest mountain range (Andes), the largest salt lake (Salar de Uyuni in Bolivia), the highest waterfall (Angel Waterfalls) and the driest place on Earth (Atacama Desert)! Well, that's plenty to be proud of!

ANTARCTICA

high point that at 4093 metres makes it the highest polar ice cap! Thanks to all the ice, Antarctica has over 70% of the world's freshwater. Did you know that if all that ice ever melted, the world's water levels would rise by 200–210 feet!

Rich no man's land!
Antarctica has territorial claims but they are not widely recognised. What a peaceful place this is. Antarctica is a no man's land rich in marine life, minerals and ore, but due to extreme weather conditions that pose grave dangers to man, not much of it has been explored.

The place!
Located on the Earth's South Pole, Antarctica is the world's fifth largest continent. Only recently it was found that this ice-covered land is not flat, but it is a mountainous terrain! The mountains and valleys are covered and filled with ice that is between 3 to 4 kilometres deep and spread over an area of 13.8 million square kilometres. It was in Antarctica that the minimum temperature ever found on Earth was recorded - a chilly -89°C!

Iceberg!
Do you know what an iceberg is? It is a large chunk of ice that has broken off from a glacier or ice shelf and is floating freely in open water. One of the biggest icebergs ever is credited to no other place but Antarctica. This 295 kilometre long and 37 kilometre wide piece of ice which had a surface area of 11,000 square kilometres above water broke free from the Ross Ice Shelf in Antarctica in 2000. It is believed

Freshwater please!
Antarctica has around 90% of the world's ice. If a place has that much ice, it is probable that it would also have some amazing facts. The highest polar ice cap is in Antarctica – Dome Argus, a vast ice plateau in east Antarctica which has a

that the under-sea dimensions of this iceberg were at least ten times of what was above water.

Creatures abound!

The most common bird in Antarctica is the penguin – an aquatic, flightless bird. Have you ever wondered why the penguins or other creatures in Antarctica don't freeze? They have special 'antifreeze' in their bodies which keeps them from being accidently frozen! In fact, thanks to the cold, a special fish found in Antarctica – the ice fish – has no haemoglobin! And they survive without it because oxygen dissolves better in cold temperatures and they manage to get their quota from that!

But the lack of haemoglobin does give them a ghostly white look!

Plant life?

You must be thinking that because of all the ice and cold, there would be no plant life in Antarctica, right? But that's not the case. Plants grow in Antarctica in the 2 percent that has ice-free periods of time. Lichens and moss grow anywhere favourable to them – in sand, soil, rock, and even on the weathered bones and feathers of dead animals! And algae, too, is found in Antarctica.

CONFUSING CAPITALS

Sure Sucre!
Did you always think that La Paz was the capital of Bolivia? Well, you weren't altogether wrong; La Paz has many administrative seats but the official capital of Bolivia is Sucre. La Paz is sometimes, erroneously, called the administrative capital of the Bolivia.

The island country!
Many have always thought that the capital of Australia was Sydney. Although it has the harbour and the Opera House and all that you think would make it an ideal capital of Australia, it is not, the capital is Canberra! In the early 20th century, there was a long debate as to whether Sydney or Melbourne should be the capital. In 1908, a compromise was reached – neither Sydney nor Melbourne but Canberra was selected as the capital of Australia.

Zealous Brazil-ous!
Similarly, if you thought Rio de Janeiro was the capital of Brazil, you were wrong. The capital of Brazil is Brasilia. From 1549 to 1763, the capital was Salvador and then from 1763 to 1960, the capital was Rio de Janeiro. The capital was shifted to Brasilia because the interiors of the country were sparsely populated and it was felt that bringing the capital there would make some difference to the population and attract people and businesses there.

largest city because that distinction has been given to Toronto. Ottawa was earlier called Bytown (from 1826 when it was founded till 1855). It got its new name in 1855 after an Algonquin word 'adawe' which means 'to trade'.

Istanbul - city of two continents

Although Istanbul (remember, it is the only city that falls on two continents – Asia and Europe) was once the seat of the Roman Empire, it is not the capital of Turkey. The capital of Turkey is Ankara. Ankara took the spot of the capital but couldn't take the spot of the largest city – it is second to Istanbul.

What's the name?

The name is not Johannesburg! Although South Africa – a country that has some of the oldest archaeological and fossil sites in the world – has three capitals, none of them is Johannesburg! Pretoria is the executive capital, Bloemfontein is the judicial capital and Cape Town is the legislative capital. Where normally one capital tends to do all of it, South Africa has clearly 'delegated' and 'divided' the role into three!

Mont-not-real!

And if you had ever thought that Montreal was the capital of Canada, you were wrong again! The capital of Canada is Ottawa. Montreal doesn't even qualify as the

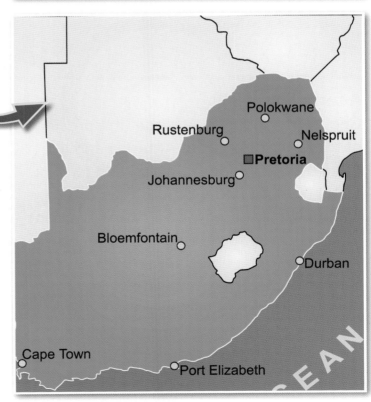

Longest serving PM!

Do you know which country's Prime Minister has served for the longest period? Singapore! Lee Kuan Yew served as the Prime Minister of Singapore from 1959 to 1990 – a record 31 consecutive years! And even when he retired, he did not get much time to stay away from politics because his son Lee Hsien Loong became prime minister and Yew became his mentor!

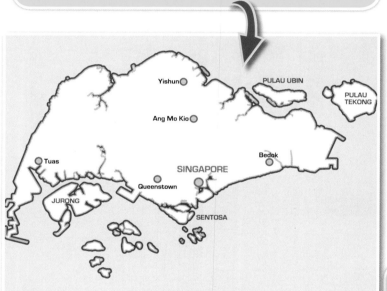

A term above all!

George Washington was the first president of the United States of America and like most other presidents, he served two terms – we all know this. But do you know who is the only American president to serve three terms? Franklin Delano Roosevelt who served from 1933 to 1945. He got elected for the fourth term also but died soon after. It was only in 1951 that a rule was made that any president could serve just two terms and no more.

Strange but true!

Henry VIII was the King of England from 1509 to 1547. Henry VIII is best known for two things – his role in the separation of the Church of England from the Roman Catholic Church and his marriages. Henry VIII married six times and the wives all had strange fates. In chronological order, he divorced Catherine of Aragon, beheaded Anne Boleyn, Jane Seymour died of natural causes, Henry VIII divorced Anne of Cleves, beheaded Catherine Howard, but Catherine Parr survived him! Divorced, beheaded, died; divorced, beheaded, lived!

Bonaparte!

Napoleon Bonaparte was the Emperor of France from 1804 to 1815. He believed that a nation that stopped complaining, stopped thinking. Quite true! Another interesting fact is that when he married his wife, he didn't like her name – Rose! He called her Josephine and the name stuck.

Richest ruler!

The richest ruler to-date is Sultan Haji Hassanal Bolkiah, the Sultan of Brunei. The sultan has the largest palace in the world with 1788 rooms and even the lavatories are inlaid with gold and silver! His planes are in silver and gold. He also has some 2000 cars! No point trying to calculate how much he is worth because we wouldn't be able to remember so many zeros!

Word it!

Whose famous words are these – 'In politics, if you want anything said, ask a man – if you want anything done, ask a woman'? These are Margaret Thatcher's words. Baroness Thatcher served as the British Prime Minister for over a decade and a half. 'The Iron Lady', as she was also knows, Margaret Thatcher led her country from 1979 to 1990.

WARS AND BATTLES

Trojan War!

What was the Trojan War? Where was it fought? The Trojan War started with the forbidden love of Paris, Prince of Troy and Helen, wife of King Menelaus of Sparta. Paris ran away with Helen and got her to Troy. The Greeks sent a fleet of ships, and an army, to get her back. That was the start of the Trojan War which lasted for 10 years. In the end, the Greeks won by a clever trick – they made a huge hollow wooden horse and placed men inside it. Then they pretended to leave Troy but when the city of Troy was sleeping the men came out of the horse and burnt the city down!

Shortest war

How short do you think the shortest war was? Some months, some weeks or some days? Not even a month, week or day, the shortest war did not even last an hour – it ended in just 38 minutes! This war was fought between Zanzibar and Britain in 1896.

And the longest!

Whereas the shortest war lasted 38 minutes, the longest war went on for much longer. It was declared in 1651 between the United Provinces of Netherlands and the Isles of Scilly. The peace treaty was signed years later, on 17th April 1986, thus ending the war between the Netherlands and Isles of Scilly 335 years after it was declared. Do you know the most interesting thing about this war – it was fought without a single shot being fired!

Roses and war?

That brings us to our next question? What was the War of the Roses? These were intermittent civil battles fought between the members of the House of Lancaster and the House of York. Shouldn't it have been called the War of the Houses then? Well, the white rose was the symbol of the House of York and the red rose was the symbol of the House of Lancaster, hence the War of the Roses.

Count again!
How long did the Hundred Years War last? 100, you think? Then you are wrong. This war that was fought between England and France (Burgundy came in later) did not last a hundred years but 116 years! Did you know that all the battles of this war were fought in France? You must be wondering how this war ended? Well, the War of the Roses left England in no position to fight in France anymore. Hence the war ended.

War in ancient times!
The Peloponnesian War was fought between Sparta and Athens between 431 and 404 B.C. In this battle, 180 Athenian triremes – meaning three oars in Latin – had to fight 170 Peloponnesian warships! Obviously, the triremes were no match for the warships and the Athenians lost and so the war ended.

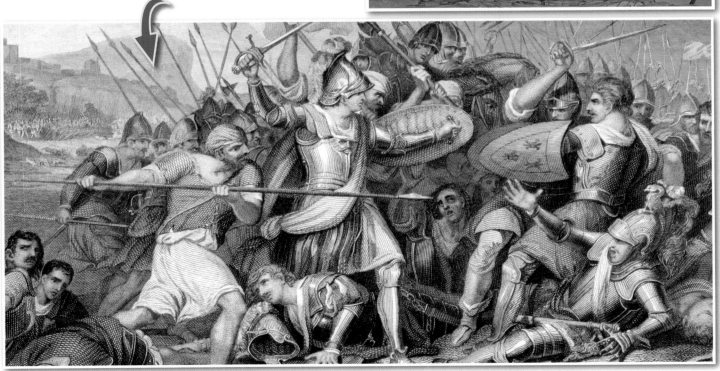

EXPLORERS

The envoy!

Marco Polo was born in 1254 in Venice. His father was a wealthy trader who travelled a lot for his business. As a youngster, Marco Polo accompanied his father to distant lands. One such journey took him to China where he met the great Kublai Khan. Kublai Khan was so impressed by the young boy that he gave him an important post in the court and soon made him an envoy. As an envoy, he travelled to various lands, some never visited by any European before. All these journeys and more are penned down in 'The Travels of Marco Polo'!

Roald Amundsen

four companions reached the South Pole. Had their arrival been delayed by another 35 days, they wouldn't have been the first because Robert Scott would have reached there first (he finally reached the South Pole on 17th January 1912). Unfortunately, he died on his way back.

Robert Edwin Peary

Poles apart!

On 6th April 1909 Robert Edwin Peary, Matthew Alexander Henson and four Eskimos became the first people to reach the North Pole. Two years later, on 14th December 1911, Roald Amundsen and his

Around the world!

In 1519, Ferdinand Magellan (1480–1521) led five Spanish ships – Trinidad, Conception, San Antonio, Victoria and Santiago – and 251 men on a journey that would later be termed as the first journey around the world. After losing three years, four ships and 233 men, only Victoria reached Spain with 18 survivors in 1522. But the man who started the journey could not return to Spain as he was killed in 1521 by the natives of the island of Mactan.

Man of many jobs!

Captain James Cook served with the British Royal Navy before taking his three renowned voyages – to Australia, New Zealand and South America. But do you know he did many odd jobs even before that? Before joining the Royal Navy, he had assisted farmers, worked at a grocer's store, and apprenticed with colliers! It was as a coal carrier in ships that Cook learned his final trade and became the thorough, systematic, professional seaman that he is most reputed for.

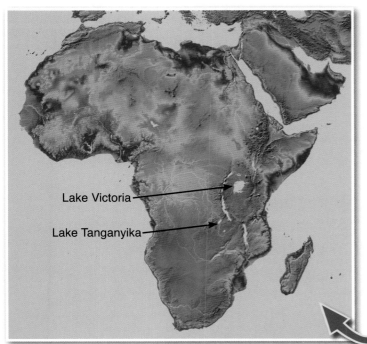

Lake Victoria

Lake Tanganyika

Name it?

Do you know the name of the second largest lake in Africa? It is also the second deepest freshwater lake in the world. Can't think of the name? It is Lake Tanganyika. Situated in the Great Rift Valley, Lake Tanganyika was discovered by Sir Richard Burton and John Hanning Speke. Speke also went on to discover Lake Victoria, which is the source of the River Nile, or so it is believed.

DISCOVERIES

A pirate, was he?

Did you know that Christopher Columbus, the man who discovered America, was a privateer –pirate working for an empire– who was entrusted with attacking Moor ships? Much later, he took to exploration. When he reached the Americas in 1492, he thought he had reached India, so he called the native people there 'Indians'. Red was added because their skin tone was reddish. Now you know why the Navajo people of America are also called Red Indians or American Indians.

So many discoveries!

Who said, 'God in the beginning created matter'? That man was none other than Sir Isaac Newton who is credited for discovering calculus and the laws of gravity. He amazingly discovered the law of gravity when an apple fell on his head and he thought why only down, why not up? Newton also built the first reflecting telescope and proved to the world that a beam of light contained all colours of the rainbow by refracting it through a prism. He was a man of many discoveries!

Water water everywhere?

It has been discovered that there is water on Mars! Who discovered water on Mars? Not one person but a team at NASA. First they figured out that the soil on Mars is similar to the soil found on some parts of Earth, and now they realise there is water there too! So, for all we know, the stories about life on Mars and aliens visiting us could be true!

Cure-it!

We know how useful radium is to us, but do you know who discovered radium or even polonium? Marie Curie, is the person known for her pioneering work in radioactivity. She was awarded the Nobel Prize for her contribution to science – in fact, she is the first person to be awarded two Nobel Prizes, one for physics and one for chemistry.

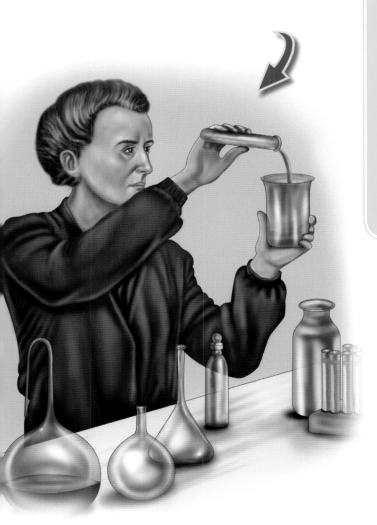

Eureka-oyancy!

Have you ever tried any water displacement activity at home, such as taking a bucket full of water and putting an object in it? What was the result? The displaced water is equal to the weight of the object. This is the law of buoyancy. This fact was discovered by Archimedes while he was having a bath in his bathtub! He got so excited that he jumped out of the tub and ran down the streets naked, shouting 'Eureka!'!

INVENTIONS

Strange patent!

Taking about patents, did you know that every country has granted patents to some whacky inventions? E Wuff got a British patent for a springboard? You might be wondering why a springboard – wait until you read more. Wuff said that the springboard would make an elephant turn somersault. But what would happen to the springboard when the elephant finally landed on it, wasn't thought of by Wuff!

Vinci the Great!

Did you know that da Vinci did a lot more than paint? He maintained many notebooks in which he had written plans for countless advanced machines for his era – air conditioners, alarm clocks, flying machines, gears, helicopters, lifebelts, parachutes, spectacles, water clocks and many more!

I am running a temperature!

How do you figure out if you have a temperature or not? With the use of a thermometer! Do you know who made the earliest version of the thermometer? Galileo Galilee (1564–1642), physicist, mathematician, philosopher and inventor who was born in Pisa, Italy. Along with the thermometer, he also invented telescopes and a compass.

Register it!

All inventions are patented so that people can't copy them and pass them off as their own. A patent is a right that is given to an inventor for a limited period during which no other person can make, use or sell an invention of the same type or name. The strange thing is that patents are territorial and are valid for the country that granted them. If another person creates the same thing in another country, no one can stop them. Did you know who was granted the first patent? Fillipo Brunelleschi in 1421 for a barge crane to transport marble!

Especially for hunters!

Have you seen any large hunting knives? They are called Bowie knives after the person who invented them – James Bowie. This knife is a lethal weapon and many people jokingly call it an Arkansas toothpick. The blade could be anywhere between 25 to 38 centimetres and to protect themselves, people would place a guard between the blade at the holder.

RAILWAYS

Can't miss this one!

When it comes to railways, you cannot help talking about the Channel Tunnel. Also known as the Euro Tunnel, the Channel Tunnel is the largest engineering project in the history of mankind. The tunnel built under the English Channel links Folkestone and Coquelles and carries many trains each day! Thanks to this tunnel, high-speed trains such as the Eurostar, which can reach a speeds of over 200 kph, can ferry passengers from London to Paris (a distance of 495 kilometres) in just two hours and fifteen minutes!

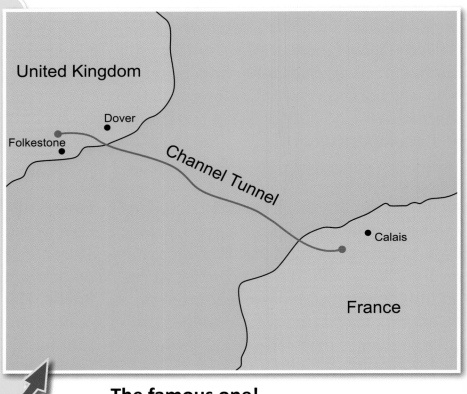

The famous one!

You must have heard of the Orient Express, the first Trans-European train. It started operating on 5th October 1883 when it made its first trip from Paris, France, to Bulgaria. From 1889, it also started trips to Istanbul (then Constantinople). It travelled across six countries until 2009 (the Istanbul route stopped operating in 1977). Why did it stop operating? Well, it became a victim of high-speed trains and low cost air travel.

Fairy!

The Fairy Queen, the oldest steam locomotive in use, was built in 1855! It was known as No. 22 when it started working for the East Indian Railways. In service until 1909, the Fairy Queen was classed an object of beauty at various sites until it was moved to the National Rail Museum in Delhi in 1972. It was brought back into service in 1997 and works as luxury train to ferry passengers between New Delhi and Alwar. When not in use, it can be seen at the National Rail Museum.

No Bumps!

Can you think of a train journey without bumps? Not possible, you think? Well, it is possible. Maglev trains (short for magnetic levitation), do not run on the track but float over it by means of magnetic repulsion. Since there is no contact between wheels and tracks, there is no friction; and in the absence of friction, there is no bump!
Imagine 'maglev-ing' on a friction-free track at speeds of up to 650 kph!

Some have some, others have more!

When it comes to railway networks, some countries are well connected, whilst others are not so well connected. For example, Djibouti, Puerto Rico, Nepal and some other places have less than 100 kilometres each of railway network. And then there are others such as the US which has some 226,427 kilometres followed by Russia which has 87,157 kilometres of track. That's quite a lot of difference between the first and the second, isn't it?

AIRCRAFT, AIRPORTS AND AIRWAYS

When last counted in August 2009, he had a collection of 1020 boarding passes! And Nick Vermeulen of the Netherlands is stranger – he loves to collect airline sick-bags. He has 6016 of them!

Faster than sound!

The only passenger aircraft to fly faster than the speed of sound is Concorde. The prototype of Concorde was displayed at the Toulouse Air Show on 11th September 1967. A year and a half later, the first French flight took place followed by many flights to countless places for many years. But in 2000 something terrible happened – the first and the only Concorde crash killed 109 people on board and four on the ground. Following an investigation, Concorde was grounded forever on 24th October 2004. You don't see Concorde in air now but you can still see them in museums.

Fancies!

What do you need a boarding pass for? Well, to board a flight! And what do you do with it once you have boarded the flight – use it as a bookmark whilst you are in the aircraft and then throw it away? Miguel Fernandez of Spain didn't throw his boarding passes away.

Terminally big!

Airports are big but how big can the biggest get? The Hong Kong International Airport passenger terminal building defies all laws of size. It is 1.3 kilometres long and covers an area of 550,000 square metres. This building, that cost $20 billion to construct, can accommodate a record 45 million people every year! With a terminal as big as that, one might want to use a car inside the terminal to travel from the baggage area to the exit!

The beginning!

When did people begin to think about flight? Probably around 400 B.C. when kites were developed in ancient China. Later, Hero of Alexandria developed the Aeolipile which used jets of steam to create rotary motion. Much later in the 15th century, Leonardo da Vinci made over 100 drawings which illustrated his theories

on flight. The 18th and 19th centuries saw the Montgolfier balloons and some early versions of Cayley's gliders. But the actual success came when the Wright Brothers developed and flew their Flyer and changed the way the world travelled!

A boat that flies?

Well, there was one. The only flight of the Hercules H-4 – also known as the Spruce Goose – took place on 2nd November 1947. The largest flying boat ever built, the Spruce Goose had a wingspan of 97.54 metres and eight engines! Howard Hughes built it for himself and flew it 20 metres above water off Long Beach in California. Does this description ring a bell? Well, it definitely would because it was recreated in the film *The Aviator*. Remember now?

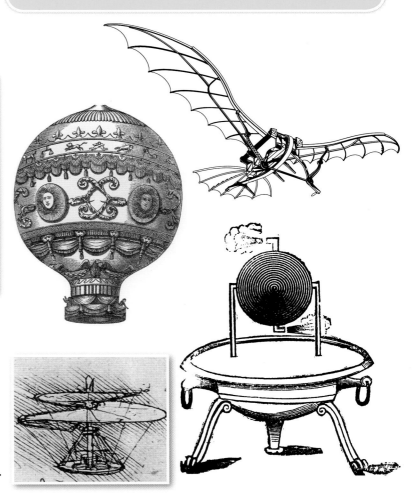

OF ROADS AND THE VEHICLES ON ROADS

Travelling in ancient times!

Have you ever wondered how people travelled in ancient times? They travelled on horseback, in carts pulled by oxen, and if they did not have any other means, they walked. Before the Romans came, there was no concept of good roads - they brought that concept with them. They used foundations of clay, chalk and gravel and put bigger flat stones on top to build remarkably straight roads. Sometimes, they made zigzagging roads as well that would make going uphill easier.

What power!

Some people have it in them and they can do anything because of their passion. Case in point is Richard Vollebregt. He left Perth in Western Australia on 13th October 2006 and travelled all the way to Sydney, New South Wales, a distance of approximately 4000 kilometres. He reached Sydney on 21st October 2006 – in 8 days, 10 hours and 57 minutes, and he made the awesome journey on a bicycle!

miles per hour! Do you want to know the price of this car? The base model starts at $ 2,400,000!

Minibike!
Why a minibike is so called is obvious, isn't it? These bikes are really mini! They are also known as mini-moto or pocket bikes. Well, they aren't that small that you can keep them in pockets, but they are very small compared to normal sized bikes. While many of us may find it difficult to ride on a pocket bike, there are some such as Ryan Galbraith and Chris Stinson who love their mini bikes so much that they travelled a record 716.58 kilometres on them in four days! They started their journey in Colorado, USA on 5th August 2009 and ended it in South Dakota, USA on 8th August 2009.

That's the limit!
And if you thought that was amazing, George Meegan of the United Kingdom left Ushuaia in Argentina on 26th January 1977 for Prudhoe Bay, Alaska. Do you know when he reached Alaska? On 18th September 2009! What was he doing all this time? Well, if you travel a distance of 30,431 kilometres on foot, it is going to take you 32 years to get there!

What's the origin?
Where does the Bugatti Veyron get its name from? From the French racing driver Pierre Veyron. He won the 24 hours Le Mans race in 1939, and it's no surprise that he was driving a Bugatti. Coming back to the present, did you know that the Bugatti Veyron Super Sport is the fastest car in the world? It can achieve a speed of 267

WATERWAYS AND WATERCRAFT

Date back?
It is difficult to give a date to the exact origin of ships and boats as we do not know anything definite, but archaeologists have found a dugout boat which dates back to 6300 B.C.! Boats with oars came in 4000 B.C., followed by sail ships in 3000 B.C. Cargo ships followed and then there was a chain of innovations and improvements – masts improved, sails improved, materials and structures improved – which finally led to the development of the amazing ships and boats that we see today.

Daring to dare!
Do you know the name of the most advanced warship? It is called HMS Daring! Belonging to the British Royal Navy, HMS Daring is a Type 45 Anti-Air warfare destroyer – the most capable air defence ship in the world. Equipped with the Principal Anti-Air Missile System (PAAMS), this ship can reach a speed of 55.5 kph in just over two minutes after being started!

What are these?
What are catamarans? These are boats with two hulls side by side. Yachts and ferries are types of catamaran. Robin Knox-Johnston, the first person to solo circumnavigate the world nonstop, under sail, did so on his yacht called Suhaili. He left Falmouth, Cornwall, UK on 14 June 1968 and returned on 22nd April 1969.

Kon-Tiki!

How did the first people travel on water? On a log! Eventually, they combined a couple of logs and made the first raft and rafts have been used ever since. Some people have used them for some strange reasons – Norwegian anthropologist Thor Heyerdahl used a raft made of balsawood called the Kon-Tiki to sail from South America across the Pacific to Polynesia in 1947. Do you know why he made the voyage? To prove that the Polynesians came from South America! So much for proving a point!

Skyscrapers?!

Where do the skyscrapers get their name from? You wouldn't believe it but the term first came from a small triangular flag that was flown from the top of a sailing ship's main mast. Then in the 19th century, people started using the term to describe tall horses and eventually tall people. Then came buildings – in the 1890's, people started calling tall buildings skyscrapers and the name has stuck ever since.

The amazing Viking ships!

Like some of us, you too may have often thought about the odd design of Viking Long ships. But contrary to what we may have thought, the length of long ships did not hinder their movement at all. In fact, thanks to the length, these ships could be used to navigate in shallow waters as well. In fact, these unique ships were known for their flatness, lightness, and speed – things that made quickly changing direction, very easy! Did you know that conquered ships were taken as souvenirs to demonstrate the naval superiority of the victor?

FILMS AND ACTORS

What is cinema?

Cinema is short for cinematography which in turn is a combination of two Greek words which mean 'movement' and 'record'. So logically, if you record a movement, it is classed as cinematography. The term was coined by the Lumière brothers, Louis and Auguste.

94,560 were paid a small fee – all this for a scene which lasted just two minutes! And what was the scene – Mohandas Karamchand Gandhi's funeral.

His name is Bond, James Bond!

Ian Fleming gave the world one of its most loved characters – James Bond. Twelve James Bond books have been made into 22 super-successful movies. But out of those 22, 20 were official and 2 were unofficial. The 'unofficial' ones were 'Casino Royale' which features David Niven as the retired James Bond and 'Never Say never Again' which was a remake of 'Thunderball'.

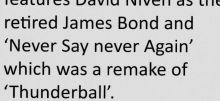

The extras!

All movies uses extras – sometimes a few and sometimes hundreds. But there are some which used many more. Gandhi, for example, used a record 294,560 extras! 200,000 of them appeared for free but

York. Many 3D movies have been made ever since, the most expensive of them being a 3D version of A Christmas Carol. But it won't be long before 3D will be old and 4D movies will be the new hit. 4D movies will have an extra dimension such as – the use of water, vibrations, smell etc. – to enhance our viewing pleasure.

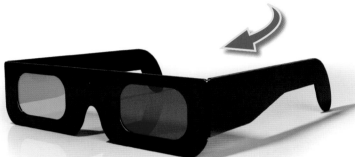

From books to movies

There are many movies – hundreds of them – that are either based on books or are inspired from them. From A Christmas Carol to Spiderman, from Batman to Harry Potter and the Chronicles of Narnia – the list is unending. The most popular of them all, as books as well as movies, is probably the Harry Potter stories!

The Oscars!

The Oscars are the most famous of the film awards and have been presented since 1929. Have you ever wondered why is it called an Oscar?

Legend has it that Margaret Hernic, who was an academy librarian, named the statuette Oscar because she thought it resemble her Uncle Oscar! The person to have the best winning streak until now is sound editor Mark Berger. He was nominated four times and took the award away every time.

From 3D to 4D!

3D movies have been a hit ever since 1915 when the first demonstration of a 3D movie was held for an audience in New

MUSIC AND MUSICIANS

Mildred J and Patty Smith Hill, wrote this song originally titled 'Good morning to you'. The words were changed much later in 1924. Did you know that the song is still in copyright and will be until 2030? But don't worry. That shouldn't stop you from singing the song at birthday parties. The copyright only applies to commercial uses.

The first!

We are so used to our mp3 players or DVD's and CD's for listening to music but have you ever thought when music was recorded for the first time? It was as long ago as 1877 when Thomas Alva Edison recorded a voice singing 'Mary had a little lamp' on a tinfoil cylinder phonograph!

The most famous song!

Well, you have sung this many times! Happy Birthday to You, Happy Birthday to You... In 1893, two American sisters,

How does it work?

Have you ever wondered how a violin works? It has a hollow wooden body and when a bow is pulled over the strings, it resonates. The violin, viola, cello and the double bass all look the same, except for their size, which gives each its own characteristic sound. The viola is larger and deeper-voiced than the violin. The cello is still larger and is played sitting down. The double bass, the largest of them all, can be played with a bow or the player can even pluck the strings.

branches – Carnatic and Hindustani. Carnatic music is more popular in south India whereas Hindustani is more popular in north and central India. Besides these classical forms, there are various folk styles that are popular in India.

The Grammy!
Why do you think the Grammy Awards were introduced? Well, rock n' roll had become so famous in the 1950's that some record executives thought that the old style music would soon die out. To keep their 'quality' music alive, they introduced the Grammy Awards. And the awards have been a hit ever since.

Classical!
When it comes to classical music, Indian music is considered to be the richest. Indian classical music is divided into two

Beat it!
When it comes to music, no description can be complete without the mention of Michael Jackson. In 2009, when he passed away, a record 11.30 million tracks were downloaded in the US and 2.8 million albums sold in the UK. He was a multiple Guinness record holder and received many awards in his lifetime. No one can ever beat the one and only, Michael Jackson.

the marathon race originates? Marathon is a place in Greece and was the place where a battle was fought between the Athenians and Persians in 490 B.C. The Athenians won and sent a messenger, Pheidippides, from Marathon to Athens to spread the news. Pheidippides covered the distance of 25 miles and conveyed the good news, but died soon after due to exhaustion. The first races were run in his honour.

Invention of baseball

Did you think baseball was an recent game? If you did, you may be wrong. Baseball was probably played in medieval times because references to ball games with bats can be seen in early manuscripts. And interestingly, a picture of 'base-ball' was published in 1744 in London. That sure makes it an old game, doesn't it?

Marathon!

We all know about a marathon race and how long it takes, but do you know how

Rings!

What do these rings means to you? Hula-hoops? No, when they are brought together they make the logo of the Olympics. The five rings can be seen on the flag which was first raised at the 1920 Antwerp Olympics. The five rings represent the five major regions of the world: Americas, Europe, Asia, Africa and Australasia. And if you look at the colours of these rings, you will be able to find at least one colour on the flag of every nation of the world. Colour perfect!

Rugby

The game of Rugby probably started in 1823. At Rugby School that year, William Web Ellis allegedly picked up a ball whilst playing football and ran with it towards the goal! The first set of Rugby rules were written around 1845 but the Rugby Football Union was formed much later in 1871 by Edwin Ash. Today the game is played by two teams each with fifteen players. The Rugby World Cup was started in 1987 and has become a global hit ever since.

Soccer! Soccer!

Do you know when the first Soccer World Cup was held? The first game of the first World Cup was played on 13th July 1930 in Uruguay. Thirteen teams participated in the first World Cup and Uruguay beat Argentina 4–2 in the final. The cup stayed in its place of birth that year! Do you know who scored the first World Cup goal? Lucien Laurent of France – nineteen minutes into the first game!

Badminton!

Have you heard of the children's game Battledore and Shuttlecock? It probably gave birth to our game of badminton. Battledore and shuttlecock was a popular game in India and other Asian countries. Battledore was a small bat that was used to hit the shuttlecock. The aim of both games is very similar – to keep the shuttle in the air for as long as possible (although badminton players try to make the other team drop the shuttlecock). When the British came to India, they loved the game but modified it by adding a net and called it 'poona'. They took the game with them to England and when they played at the Duke of Beaufort's house in 1873, the Duke renamed the game badminton after his house 'Badminton House'.

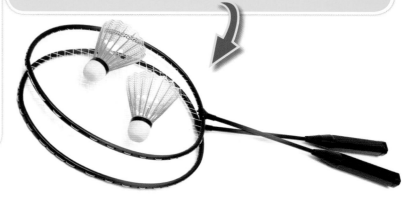

LANGUAGE AND COMMUNICATION

The beginning

From cave paintings to stone tablets, it has been a long journey for mankind. Conveying ideas was the objective and people would use one method or another to communicate. Pictographs were the first method which eventually led to the alphabet. Code sent via Telegraph was a breakthrough because finally, the use of messengers to carry information was no longer necessary.

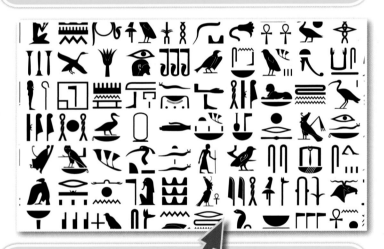

Hieroglyphics

The simplest way to communicate is by using pictures, such as the ones that you see on road signs or even computer icons. But telling a story was a lengthy task, so people started using hieroglyphics, a simple version of images. Hieroglyphics use symbols that represent an object, an idea or a sound. People stopped using hieroglyphics in the 1st century AD and attempts to read them were made only in 1822 when the Rosetta Stone was found.

A	B	C	D	E	F
· −	− · · ·	− · − ·	− · ·	·	· · − ·
G	H	I	J	K	L
− − ·	· · · ·	· ·	· − − −	− · −	· − · ·
M	N	O	P	Q	R
− −	− ·	− − −	· − − ·	− − · −	· − ·
S	T	U	V	W	X
· · ·	−	· · −	· · · −	· − −	− · · −
Y	Z				
− · − −	− − · ·				

Code it!

What is communication? In simple words: the conveying of thoughts from one person to another. In 19th century, Samuel Finley Breese Morse created the

Morse Code – a system of dots and dashes – to send messages. Morse code has five parts – a dot, a dash, a short gap (between letters), a medium gap (between words) and a long gap (between sentences). Here's the Morse alphabet for you. Morse away your evening!

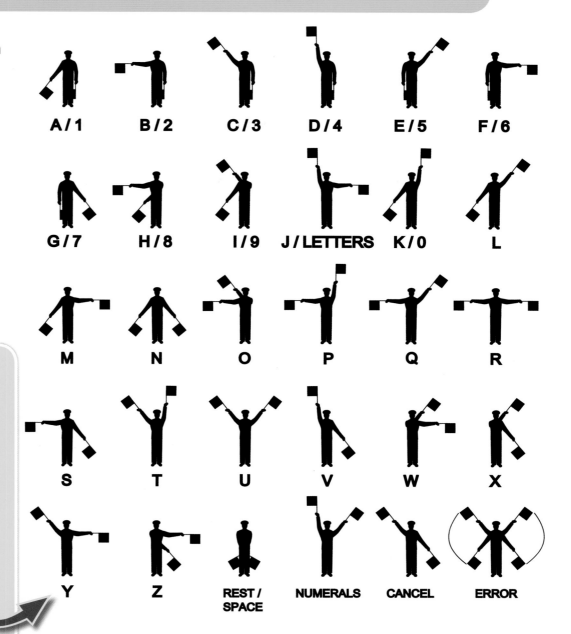

A / 1 B / 2 C / 3 D / 4 E / 5 F / 6

G / 7 H / 8 I / 9 J / LETTERS K / 0 L

M N O P Q R

S T U V W X

Y Z REST / SPACE NUMERALS CANCEL ERROR

Semaphore!

Semaphore flags is a way of signalling that was developed by French inventor Claude Chappe and his brothers. This system used two wooden arms which could be set to seven different positions. A total of 196 combinations were created to send messages. The signalling device was placed on a high building and the receiver could use a telescope to view the message. This system was used until the 1960's, long after radio signals had started being used.

Sign language

Why do you rub your stomach when you feel hungry? Or give a thumbs up to say yes or all OK? Or stick your tongue out to tease someone? This is called sign language – a language where you do not use words but signs to communicate your feelings to others. Sign language is mostly used by deaf people. The first instance of this was in Europe in the 17th century.

ARCHITECTS, ENGINEERS AND BUILDINGS

Bird's nest!

We're not talking about a real bird's nest but the Beijing Olympic Stadium designed by Swiss architects Herzog and de Meuron. It is the largest steel structure ever built and cost $423 million. The main body is a saddle-shaped elliptical steel structure weighing 38,100 tonnes.

Tallest ever!

The Burj Khalifa, formally known as Burj Dubai, is not only the tallest manmade structure but also the tallest building ever. 828 metres tall, this building, which opened in Dubai in January 2009, has a record 160 storeys! And there goes another award to Burj Dubai for the building with most floors ever. Dubai seems to have a knack for tall structures. The tallest hotel, the Rose Rayhaan; and the world's largest shopping centre, the Dubai Mall, are also in Dubai.

101!

Taipei 101 building has 101 floors. Until the Burj Dubai took over the record, it was the tallest building in the world. Taipei 101 has two of the fastest lifts in the world which cover 1010 metres in an minute. Considering this building is around 500 metres tall, you would be on top floor in 30 seconds! In 2004, Alain Robert climbed the outside of Taipei 101 and it took him four hours to get to the top. Well done, 'Spiderman'.

20th century, London Bridge needed to be replaced by a newer one, so American businessman Robert P McCulloch bought it for $2,460,000! It was dismantled, shipped to the US and assembled in Lake Havasu City, Arizona. It would seem like a whimsical buy to many but this made it the largest structure ever moved and the largest antique ever sold.

Permanently temporary!

Did you know that the Eiffel Tower was built as a temporary structure for the Universal Exhibition held in Paris in 1889? It became so popular that it was not destroyed after. It took its named from the man who created it – Gustave Eiffel. What other famous structure did he create? The Statue of Liberty, which was created in France and sent to the US as a gift!

London bridge is falling down!

It did not fall down but was 'dismantled' stone by stone and taken to the US! In the

Buried with a word?

Where does the word mausoleum come from? From Mausolus, an ancient Persian ruler, who ruled a part of the Persian Empire from 377 to 353 B.C. His widow built a magnificent tomb for him at Halicarnassus. The Mausoleum was damaged in an earthquake and what remained was destroyed in 1522. This 'great tomb' called the Mausoleum gave birth to the word.

ART AND ARTISTS

David!
The famous statue of David was created between 1501 and 1504. It was installed outside Palazzo della Signoria in Florence in 1504 and stayed there until 1873 when it was moved to Accademia Gallery to protect it from damage. Its absence became so noticed that a replica was later placed at the Palazzo. You must be wondering who carved the statue of David? The answer is Michelangelo. Did you know that Michelangelo had a tough time convincing the authorities that he could carve the statue because he was only 26 at the time!

Flying da Vinci!
Leonardo da Vinci was one of the greatest artists of all time. He was not only the painter of 'Mona Lisa' and the 'Last Supper' and various other renowned paintings, but he was also a scientist and engineer. His inventions and mechanical drawings have been the starting point for many researchers. Did you know that before the Wright Brothers created the first aircraft, Da Vinci had made a drawing of a flying craft? Da Vinci, like all the other artists of his time, was also known to dissect dead bodies! Why? To research and study anatomy for his drawings.

Where is it screaming?
Who is screaming? We are referring to the painting – The Scream – which was made by Edvard Munch in 1893. Edvard made several versions of his painting. The one that was

hung at the National Gallery in Oslo was stolen in 1994 and held for ransom. It was recovered without the ransom being paid. Then another one hung at the Munch Museum was stolen by armed thieves in 2004. It is still missing to this day! Next time you see this painting (an original and not a replica), then you know to report it!

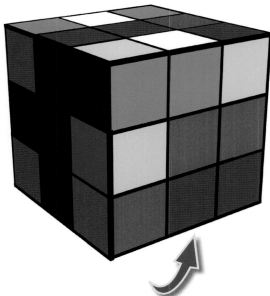

Rubik's cube!
What do you do with a Rubik's cube? Play and twist it, straining your brain to match colours on one side, and wondering how people make it look easy! Well, not everyone uses them this way – five artists from Canada got together, with 4050

Rubik's cubes and recreated a mosaic of the Last Supper! The Guinness Book of records it as the largest of its kind!

The survivor!
The oldest figurative sculpture is a figurine that was carved out of a mammoth's tusk in around 33,000 B.C. It is called the Venus of Hohle Fels because it was discovered in the Hohle Fels cave near Ulm in Baden-Wurttemberg, Germany. This figure was discovered as recently as 2008 by a team at the University of Tubingen headed by Nicholas Conrad.

Sand lovers!
Do you love playing with sand and making castles? Jim Denevan of the USA loves it too; so much so that he created the largest sand art ever in May 2009. How large was it? Well, if something is 4.86 kilometres in diameter, you can imagine how large it would be! His art contained over 1000 individual circles!

Yachting!

Why is a yacht called a yacht? Because in Dutch, 'jacht' (from which it is derived) means to hunt and this light ship was used to 'hunt' pirates and other transgressors. But a yacht's status has increased since those days. Today, it is an indication of wealth and fame. Roman Abramovich, the owner of the Chelsea Football Club owns a yacht, Eclipse, which is 560 feet long and is estimated to be worth $ 485 million!

The first!

The first dollar billionaire was John D Rockefeller. To be a billionaire in the late 19th and early 20th century was no easy feat. But Rockefeller invested in oil and managed to become a man worth every penny – $ 1.4 billion! Researchers have estimated that if the money that he had back then was taken and converted to today's dollar (with inflation) his bank balance would be around $ 210 billion making him the richest man ever! To his credit, Rockefeller gave away a large part of his fortune to very worthy causes. He sure was a worthy billionaire.

Teaching business!

Do you know the name of America's oldest university in the world? It is also the wealthiest university in the world. The oldest in America and the wealthiest university in the world is Harvard University located in Cambridge, Massachusetts. It was established in 1636 and Harvard's endowment was around $ 26 billion!

Not right!
Well, it doesn't always help to be extremely rich. Sometimes it backfires, as it did in the case of an unknown Swiss millionaire who was fined $ 290,000 for speeding! That's a lot of money to go over the limit by 57 kph! But the police felt that being a 'wealthy and persistent' traffic offender, that's the least that man should have paid. After all, it was for the love of his red Ferrari Testarossa!

Richest author!
And when it comes to money in billions, how can we forget the first billion-dollar author J K Rowling. Her Harry Potter series has taken her to heights unknown and unachieved by anyone in the past. Did you know that many publishers rejected her first manuscript saying that such fantasy wouldn't sell? Too bad for them, because Harry Potter books have sold 400 million copies all over the world and have been published in more than 55 languages!

Rich Anglo Saxons!
Some Anglo Saxons must have been extremely wealthy. How do we know? If a farmer in Staffordshire could bury 650 items of gold and 530 silver items around the 7th century, then he surely would have been rich! This treasure was discovered by metal detection specialist Terry Herbert of the UK.

HUMAN BODY

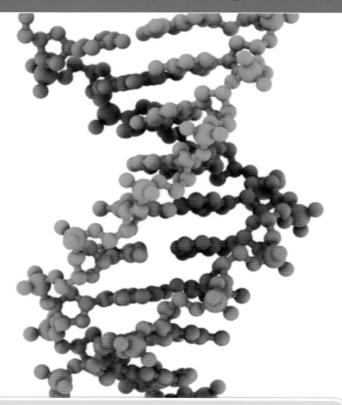

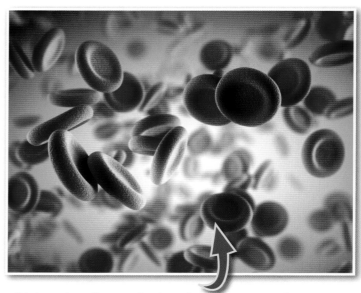

of blood cells and platelets. Do you know that our blood cells take only 60 seconds to complete one circuit of the body?

Complex machine!

The most complex and complicated machine in the world is the human body. For a very long time the working of the body was unknown to us, but more recently scientists have uncovered many interesting secrets. The most important of all the discoveries so far is that of DNA molecules – the basic structure of life! It is interesting to know that our body makes billions of cells every day and every new cell copies the genetic information from the nucleus – copying something that complex would normally take around 95 years, our body does in 6–8 hours!

Our survival kit!

How much blood do you think you have in your body? Almost 5 litres in men (4.3 litres in women)! Blood is a connective fluid which is made up of 55% of plasma and 45%

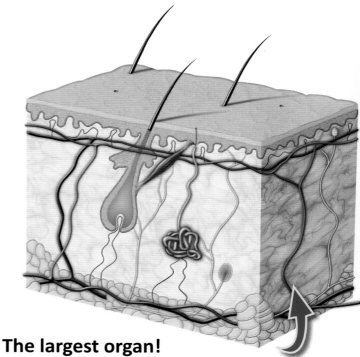

The largest organ!

The largest organ of our body is the skin. So large that it covers an area of around 1.8 square metres and contributes to around 4 kilograms to your body weight. Do you know we shed almost 50,000 flakes every minute? That amounts to around 18 kilograms in a person's lifetime! Another interesting thing to know is that around 80% of your house dust is nothing but skin flakes!

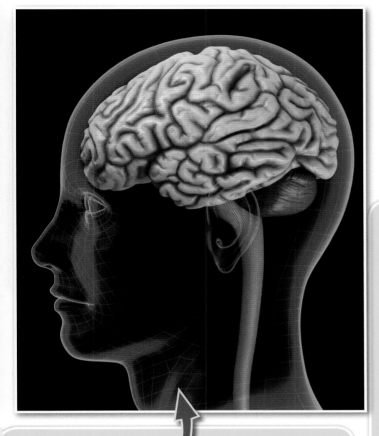

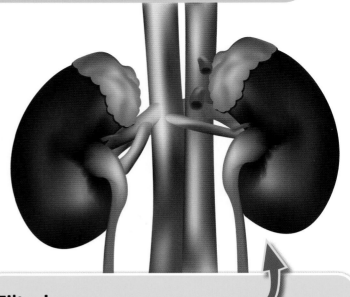

Filter!
Our kidneys aren't big — each kidney is about 4.5 inches long and weighs round 4–6 ounces. They are the best filters a body can have — they each contain around one million individual filters! They filter almost 1.3 litres of blood per minute and help to excrete around 0.5–2 litres urine per day (depending upon liquid intake, temperature, body size etc.)

The power!
What gives us all the power to think and work? What controls our actions and moods? What helps all of our body organs to function properly? Our brain! Even though we lose 100,000 brain cells in the first years of our life, the remaining grand total of 100 billion cells keeps us going a lifetime.

Hearty issues!
The heart looks like this and not like the shape you see elsewhere! The heart is a very active organ (more than the other organs) and pumps 13,640 litres of blood around our body every day! This 11 ounce organ can create enough energy to drive a truck for twenty miles every day. How much would that make in a lifetime - a trip to the moon and back?

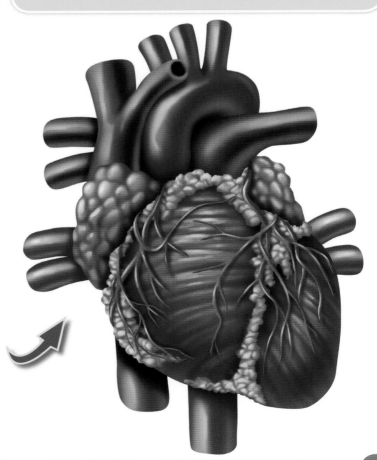

VIKINGS AND PIRATES

Who were they?

Who were the Vikings? Vikings were raiders from three Scandinavian countries – Denmark, Norway and Sweden – who travelled between 700 and 1100 to countries such as Britain and Ireland to loot and plunder. Unlike other looters, Vikings plundered many monasteries and churches because they were pagans and did not believe in Christianity.

The journey after life!

Some Vikings were considered very important, so much so that when they died, they were placed in a burial ship along with all their belongings – clothes, jewellery and even pets – and the ship was set alight and pushed out to sea. As an alternative to setting it alight, they covered the ship with huge amounts of earth so that it sank.

Name game!

Where do the Vikings get their name from? From a language called Old Norse. In Old Norse, Viking meant 'pirate raid'. Every time people went raiding in ships, they were said to have 'gone Viking'. Vikings in some countries were popular – the Byzantine emperors in Constantinople hired them as guards! They were called Varangian Guards.

it is believed that he had buried a lot of treasure somewhere and was killed by Maynard because of this. But Maynard couldn't find any clue about the location of the treasure so the secret died with him.

The Jolly Roger!
This is a Jolly Roger flag – a skull with two bones forming an cross below it. A flag of this kind on a ship means that it is a pirate ship! This flag was designed to be scary, whether or not it achieved this, is difficult to say! Although 'designed' only for pirates, it was also used by people travelling in the Spanish Main.

What was he 'Teaching'?
Edward Teach, you would probably recognise the name Blackbeard, was a famous British pirate. He was a privateer before he switched to being a pirate and

The eye-patch!
The eye-patch is often associated with pirates but that's not really fair. Even ordinary sailors wore eye-patches. There is no doubt that some pirates would have worn eye-patches (they could have lost an eye in a fight) but it wasn't a trend or costume! The image was made popular by media culture – movies and books!

WORLD RELIGIONS

Ancient religions

In most ancient civilizations, people did not believe in just one god but many gods. Gods had special characteristics and each god was associated with a function. Almost every ancient religion had gods with similar responsibilities. For example, Guan-yu was the Chinese god of war, Month was the Egyptian god of war, Baluchabtan was the Mayan god of war, Ares was the Greek god of war, Mars was the Roman god of war, and Thor was the Norse god of war.

Greek or Roman?

Have you noticed that the ancient Romans had the same gods as the ancient Greeks, but their names were different? It is believed that the ancient Romans copied the ancient Greek set of Gods and only Apollo got to keep the same name in both civilizations. Here's a list of what the Greek gods were called in Rome:

Greek	Roman
Aphrodite	Venus
Apollo	Apollo
Ares	Mars
Artemis	Diana
Athena	Minerva
Demeter	Ceres
Hades	Pluto
Hephaistos	Vulcan
Hera	Juno
Hermes	Mercury
Hestia	Vesta
Kronos	Saturn
Persephone	Proserpina
Poseidon	Neptune
Zeus	Jupiter

Hinduism

Hinduism is the oldest religion in the world, in fact, it is not a religion but a way of life. There are four books known as the Vedas which contain the earliest Hindu beliefs and principles. You can also find the influence of the Vedas on Sikhism, Buddhism and Jainism. Two epic poems, the Mahabharata and the Ramayana, set out the basics of the Hindu philosophy – selflessness, duty, devotion and meditation.

Many followers!

Christianity has the most number of followers. The sacred book of Christians – the Bible – is written in two parts, the Old Testament and the New Testament. There are many animals that are talked about in the Bible; sheep and lambs are talked about the most, probably due to their importance for wool and meat. Lions also find a mention a number of times probably because they were a symbol of power, strength and wisdom.

Islam

After Christianity, Islam has the most followers. Believers of Islam are called Muslims who believe in Allah and the Prophet Muhammad, his messenger, who revealed his messages to the world. Their holy book is called the Qur'an. Mecca and Medina are holy places for Muslims and so are Jerusalem and Karbala.

us to do just that. From 1 to 10 are fairly common, but 11 and above are disasters! Here's the list from 0-12.

Wind	Wind speed
Calm air	0–2 kph
Light air	3–6 kph
Slight breeze	7–11 kph
Gentle breeze	12–19 kph
Moderate breeze	20–28 kph
Fresh breeze	29–38 kph
Strong breeze	39–49 kph
High wind	50–61 kph
Gale	62–74 kph
Strong gale	75–88 kph
Whole gale	89–102 kph
Storm	103–117 kph
Hurricane	Over 118 kph

Cloudy start!

We love looking at the clouds, don't we? Do you find shapes in the clouds like most of us? But have you ever thought beyond just the shape of the clouds? There are ten types of clouds – stratus, cumulus, stratocumulus, cumulonimbus (which appear between 450–2000 metres), nimbostratus (which appear between 900–3000 metres), altostratus, altocumulus (which appear between 2000–7000 metres), cirrus, cirrostratus and cirrocumulus (which appear between 5000–13,500 metres).

From breeze to hurricane!

A gentle breeze is a wind and a hurricane is also a wind so how do we distinguish between the two. The Beaufort scale helps

Charging!
Why does lightning occur? Lightning is an electrostatic discharge that happens during thunderstorms, or after dust storms or volcanic activity. Lightning is always accompanied by thunder. Lightning can either be negative or positive which means that it can either negatively or positively charge the earth. Positive lightning is stronger than negative lightning and can strike with a billion volts and with currents reaching 300,000 amperes!

Disaster this?!
What's missing from the list above? The deadly tornado! Tornadoes, or twisters, are deadly winds that blow at speeds of up to 420 kph. These are so deadly that they can not only destroy crops but also houses and vehicles. You might even find cows and other animals swirling in air!

Port wave!
What does that mean? Well, its a tsunami! In Japanese, 'tsu' means port and 'nami' means wave. So, a huge wave that hits a port is a tsunami. These huge wall-like structures are created when an earthquake occurs under the ocean floor. In some cases tsunamis occur due to volcanic activity under the sea. The deadliest tsunami to date is that which hit south east Asia in December 2004.

NATURAL DISASTERS!

date was the Great Chilean earthquake of 22nd May 1960. It measured 9.5 on Richter scale.

Disastrous!

What's the difference between a cyclone and a hurricane? None! A cyclone is another name for a hurricane. The most disastrous cyclone to date was Hurricane Katrina that destroyed the coast of Louisiana and its surrounding states on 29th August 2005. It has been estimated that damage amounted to $156 billion! That made it one of the costliest natural disasters in the United States!

Quaking and shivering!

There are plates that form the surface of the Earth and these are called tectonic plates. Tectonic plates are slowly moving but we don't feel their movement on a daily basis. When we do feel them is if there is a sudden slip or jolt. The resulting earthquakes can shake entire buildings and cause a lot of damage to lives and property. The most powerful earthquake to

Muddy affair!

What harm can mud do? Not much you'd think, but that's not the case. In December 1999, 35 inches of rain in Vargas state in Venezuela caused mudslides which resulted in between 10,000–30,000 deaths! Many building, roads and entire towns were wiped out, buried under mud!

Sliding down!

What happens when you slide down a snowy slope? When you start sliding, a little amount of snow falls with you but as you go down further, the snow picks up more snow and by the end of it there is a lot of snow that lands with you at the bottom. This is how an avalanche is made. It starts with a small ball that picks up more and more snow as it falls down, and we all know what the end result is! The worst avalanche disaster to date was the 'Winter of Terror' a period when there was a series of 649 avalanches that rolled

Hot hot hot!

Can you tolerate the heat? It's difficult for some people to tolerate the heat, and many couldn't tolerate the hot August of 2003 which was considered to be the hottest ever summer in the northern hemisphere. Temperatures reached 40°C and as many as 35,000 (some reports say 52,000) people perished in this hot spell.

down the Swiss, Australian and Italian Alps. Estimates say that at least 45,000 people were affected by this series of avalanches.

Fire in the wild!

A wildfire is an uncontrolled fire in any sort of vegetation or forest. Lightning, volcanic eruption or even spontaneous spark can lead to an uncontrolled forest fire. The worst ever wildfire was the Peshtigo tragedy which destroyed around 3800 kilometres of forest and farmland around Wisconsin and Michigan on 8th October 1871. You must be wondering why it was named the Peshtigo tragedy – because half the population of Peshtigo village died.

GLOBAL WARMING

What is global warming?

That's a simple question with a simple answer: the average temperature of our land and seas is increasing every year and is continuing in an upward trend. That's global warming in simplest terms. But the impact of global warming is not as simple as the explanation. Global warming at its current rate is threatening the existence of many species.

What can you do?

Many countries and organisations are doing a lot to increase awareness about global warming, and in turn, control it. You can also do your bit by following the three R's – reduce, reuse and recycle. Reduce the consumption of electricity (switch off the lights and fans when you leave your room), reduce water wastage (turn off the tap while you are brushing); reuse old bags (don't throw something away if it is old - use it or donate), try to use products that cannot be recycled and recycle whatever can be recycled (the best way to start is by separating rubbish into what can and can't be recycled so that they can be placed in their respective bins.

Animals in danger

Global warming is threatening many different creatures, plants and animals. Some can adapt and survive, but others can't and have died and many more are on the brink of extinction. Imagine how bad it would be if you wouldn't be able to see your favourite animal or plant? And remember Nemo (of Finding Nemo fame)? He was a clownfish and those are also in danger. We might be searching for Nemo but never be able to find him if we don't do something about global warming!

Plants!

It is not only animals that are in danger, many plants and trees are in danger too. Some are not only in danger because of global warming, they are being threatened by man cutting them down! The more trees are cut, the more global warming will increase; and the more global warming increases, the more trees will die every year! It's a vicious circle – and only we can break it!

What has led to this?

We cannot pinpoint just one thing that has led to global warming. It is a combination of many activities that has brought us to this point. The biggest culprit is fossil fuels which we use in cars, planes, in heavy machinery and factories and electricity production for our homes as well as businesses! This is compounded by chemical waste, deforestation and many other things.

Save the world

It is our duty to do whatever we can to save our world and the lovely plants and animals that live in our world. Whatever small things that we already do, there is one major thing that all of us should do – plant trees! Reforestation is the key to saving the world.

TIME FOR RANDOM FACTS!

on 16th June 1936, Ernestine is the oldest bodybuilder in the world.

Iron iron!
Iron on my feet! A lot of metal on your feet (or even a medium amount) will ensure that you can't walk a step. But not for Zhang Zhenghui, a physical fitness freak! Zhenghui wore cast iron shoes weighing 122.8 kilograms and walked for 10 metres!

Fire! Fire!
Fire can burn but some people still love to play with fire. Don't believe me? On the 25th February 2010, Ted Batchelor endured a burn – a full body burn – for a record 2 minutes 57 seconds, and that was without oxygen. It's not a surprise that Ted is a stuntman.

Body building!
Body building is fun. It is a passion for some people and necessity for others! And for some it is an addiction. Ernestine Shepherd feels strongly about it, if at over 75 years she is still body building! Born

Strawing!
What would you do with these straws? Drink cola or make a straw house or try to make a long pipe from it? Simon Elmore of Germany thought differently. When given 400 straws, he held them all in his mouth for a record ten seconds!

Can you break this one?
You love pasta, don't you? Ernesto Cesario loves pasta so much that he ate a 150 gram bowl of it in 1 minute 30 seconds. He is a record holder when it comes to eating pasta – do you want to try to break this record?

Pulling an aircraft!
You may have sat on this plane or a one similar to it. But have you ever thought of pulling it? Probably not , but someone has. Rev. Kevin Fast of Canada pulled a Globemaster III which weighs 188.83 tonnes! He managed to pull it a record 8.8 metres on 17th September 2009.

MULTIPLE CHOICE

1. **What is the name of the largest known asteroid?**

- Amos
- Berg
- Berry
- Ceres

2. **The Andromeda Galaxy is ------------------ light years away from Earth.**

- 2,309,000
- 2,310,219
- 2,785,641
- 2,984,554

3. **What is the official name of Xena?**

- Eric
- Eris
- Erik
- Erix

4. **Which animal can die if given the drug penicillin?**

- Mouse
- Guinea Pig
- Cat
- Dog

5. **Who is Venus known as in Greek mythology?**

- Hera
- Aphrodite
- Athena
- Medusa

6. **The longest snake in the world is _____.**

- Anaconda
- Viper
- Reticulated python
- Cobra

7. **How many million years does the Sun take to complete one orbit around the centre of our galaxy?**

- 200–225
- 225–250
- 250–275
- 275–300

8. In which year were the twin cities of Pompeii and Herculaneum buried under ash and lava when Mount Vesuvius erupted?

- A.D. 73
- A.D. 75
- A.D 77.
- A.D. 79

9. Sarv-e-Abarkooh, a national monument of Iran, belongs to which family of trees?

- Ficus
- Redwood
- Cypress
- Oak

10. What is the largest flying bird?

- Ostrich
- Bustard
- Eagle
- Pterosaur

11. In the Iliad, who does Homer talk about at length?

- Odysseus
- Achilles
- Zeus
- Heracles

12. Name the youngest state of America.

- Alaska
- Colorado
- Hawaii
- Wyoming

13. The typical pirate flag – a skull with two crossed bones below it – is known as _____.

- Roger Lilly
- Jolly Roger
- Jolly Rapper
- Rapper Billy

14. Which of these were used to make moving components of watches in old days?

- Square fungus
- Bracket fungus
- Rectangle fungus
- Circle fungus

15. What is the oldest religion in the world?

- Christianity
- Hinduism
- Islam
- Judaism

MULTIPLE CHOICE

16. How old is our solar system?

- 3.5 billion years
- 4 billion years
- 4.56 billion years
- 5 billion years

17. Which out of these is a marsupial?

- Bat
- Echidna
- Whale
- Koala

18. How many languages are spoken in Africa?

- 1000
- 2000
- 3000
- 4000

19. Birds shed their feathers at intervals and grow new ones. What is this process called?

- Melting
- Moulting
- Malting
- Milting

20. When was the first Soccer World Cup played?

- 1925
- 1930
- 1935
- 1940

21. Which is the tallest building in the world?

- Dubai Mall
- Dubai Star
- Burj Dubai/Khalifa
- Rose Rayhaan

22. The Incas died out when the_____ invaded their lands.

- French
- German
- Portuguese
- Spanish

23. It was only recently discovered that _____ is a mountainous terrain!

- Antarctica
- Arctic

- Alaska
- Greenland

24. What is the Japanese puffer fish called?

- Naki naki
- Maki maki
- Saki saki
- Laki laki

25. What is the name of the tree under which Buddha got enlightenment?

- Buddha tree
- Buddhi tree
- Bodhi tree
- Barhi tree

26. The largest waterfall in the world is _____.

- Victoria Falls
- Niagara Falls
- Angel Falls
- Tugela Falls

27. Name the only city that falls over two continents?

- Istanbul
- Barsa
- Manisa

- Ankara

28. In whose praise was the Colossus of Rhodes made?

- Zeus
- Hades
- Helios
- Achilles

29. Which of these has the most number of geysers?

- Kruger National Park
- Yellowstone National Park
- Grand Canyon National Park
- Denali National Park

30. The script of the _____ has not been deciphered yet.

- Sumerian Civilization
- Ancient Egyptian Civilization
- Ancient Greek Civilization
- Indus Valley Civilization

31 Which disease in the Middle Ages was popularly referred to as 'Black Death'?

- Malaria
- Bubonic plague
- Whooping cough
- Tuberculosis

MULTIPLE CHOICE

32. Which is the only god to keep the same name in both Greek and Roman civilizations?

- Apollo

- Zeus

- Aphrodite

- Vulcan

32. How many brain cells are lost in the early years of life on an average?

- 50,000

- 100,000

- 150,000

- 200,000

33. Which is the oldest university in USA?

- Massachusetts Institute of Technology

- Harvard University

- Stanford University

- Purdue University

34. Which is the longest mountain range in the world?

- The Sierra Nevada

- The Andes

- The Himalayas

- The Alps

35. Which is the largest flower species in the world?

- Rafflesia

- Titan Arum

- Giant Amazon water lily

- Edelweiss

36. Which bear eats about 38 percent of its own weight of food a day?

- Sloth bear

- Black bear

- Polar bear

- Panda bear

37. In terms of intelligence, which animal comes after humans?

- Gorilla

- Chimpanzee

- Baboon

- Gibbon

38. The Great Chilean earthquake of May 1960 measured ------ on Richter scale?

- 8.5

- 9

- 9.5

- 10

39. Which is the largest fish family with over 2000 species?

- Puffer fish

- Clown fish

- Goby fish

- Swordfish

40. Which insect's name in German translates to 'little biter'?

- Beetle

- Ant

- Wasp

- Spider

41. What are clouds that appear between 900 and 3000 meters called?

- Cirrostratus

- Cirrus

- Nimbostratus

- Cirrocumulus

42. Who discovered the most number of asteroids?

- Edmond Halley

- Galileo Galilee

- Eugene Shoemaker

- Edward Hubble

43. Which is the brightest star apart from Sun that can be seen from Earth?

- Cygnus OB2-12

- Sirius

- Canopus

- Alpha Centauri

44. In Egyptian mythology, who was depicted as a falcon-headed God?

- Set

- Isis

- Horus

- Tefnut

Curriculum Visions

Musli...
holy days

Lisa Magloff

Glossary

ARABIC The language spoken by Mohammed (pbuh), and so the language the Qur'an was written in. Not all Muslims speak Arabic, but many try to learn it.

EMIGRATION (HIJIRAH) The time, in 622, when Mohammed (pbuh) and his followers were forced to flee Mecca and go to Medina.

FAST A period of going without food. During Ramadan, healthy adult Muslims fast from sunrise to sunset every day. Remember that because the Muslim holy days move throughout the entire year over time, in some years Ramadan occurs in the summer, when days are very long.

HAJJ A pilgrimage, or trip, to Mecca that is taken by millions of Muslims at a certain time of each year. The purpose of the Hajj is for Muslims to worship at the Ka'ba and to re-dedicate themselves to God at important sites. It is the goal of every Muslim to make the trip at least once in a lifetime. The Hajj is immediately followed by the festival of Eid al-Adha.

IFTAR Every day during Ramadan, the fast is broken at sunset with a meal called iftar.

IMAM An imam is a religious scholar or someone very knowledgeable about Islam who leads the congregational prayers.

IMAM HUSSAIN The grandson of Mohammed (pbuh). He was killed in 680 CE during a battle over who should lead the Muslims. Some Muslim traditions honour Hussain for his courage and willingness to stand up for what he felt was right.

ISLAM The religion followed by Muslims. The word Islam means 'Submission to God'.

KA'BA The cube-shaped structure in Mecca towards which all Muslims pray. Muslims believe that the Ka'ba was first built by Adam and rebuilt by Abraham according to God's instructions.

MAWLID A festival, usually in honour of the birthday of Mohammed (pbuh) or another important Muslim.

MOSQUE The Muslim place of worship and prayer. Muslims can worship anywhere, but believe there is special value in worshipping together at the mosque whenever they can.

MOHAMMED (PBUH) The founder of Islam. To Muslims he is the last Messenger of God to humanity and the last prophet in a line which included Abraham, Noah, Moses and Jesus.

PROPHET A person who delivers a message from God to humanity. Muslims believe there were many prophets, including Abraham, Moses and Jesus, but that Mohammed (pbuh) was the last.

QUR'AN The holy book of Islam. Muslims believe that it contains the exact word of God and was given by God to Mohammed (pbuh) bit-by-bit over many years.

TARAWEEH Special evening prayers performed during Ramadan. During each night's prayer, one thirtieth of the Qur'an is recited, so that by the end of the month the entire Qur'an is read out loud. The taraweeh is often recited by people who have memorised the entire Qur'an.

Contents

As you go through the book, look for words in **BOLD CAPITALS**. These words are defined in the glossary.

 Understanding others

Remember that other people's beliefs are important to them. You must always be considerate and understanding when studying about faith.

Worshippers at an outdoor service.

3

What is a holy day?

Muslim holy days celebrate the teachings and life of the prophet Mohammed (pbuh) and events in the Islamic holy book.

People of all faiths worship throughout the whole year. For example, many Muslims pray five times a day, every day of the week. These prayers may take place in the MOSQUE, at home, at work or school. On Fridays, many Muslims go to the mosque for special worship services. Friday is called Yawm al-Jumu'ah, or 'Day of Congregation'.

But in all faiths, some days are special. These special days, or holy days, may remember an important event in the history of the faith, or they may be written about in holy writings, or scripture.

These special days involve public celebrations, festive meals, festivals and even processions. In general, we call these special days holy days and it is from this that we get the word 'holiday'.

Some of these days and times celebrate important events in the life of the PROPHET MOHAMMED (PBUH), other holy days remember and celebrate teachings in the Muslim holy book, the QUR'AN.

As you look at the main holy days of the Muslim faith in this book, notice how each day is marked out or celebrated in a different way. Some holy days are happy and joyous times, and others are times to be solemn and quiet. All Muslim holy days involve prayer, but some are also celebrated with festivals and community processions, while others are celebrated with solemn worship services.

Arabic words

You will notice quite a few **ARABIC** words in this book. Because **ISLAM** began in Arabia, and the Holy Qur'an is written in Arabic, most Muslims speak some Arabic. So, most Muslims also use the Arabic names of the holidays, and some other common Arabic words, not their English translation.

pbuh

This stands for Peace be unto Him, and is a sign of respect accorded to the prophet Mohammed (pbuh) whenever his name is written.

◀ These people are celebrating the birthday of the Prophet Mohammed (pbuh) with Islamic songs and a special type of religious dancing. The music and dancing helps to bring people closer to God.

Weblink: www.CurriculumVisions.com

The Muslim holy day calendar

Here are the parts of the year when Muslim holidays occur. The actual date varies from one year to another.

The Muslim Calendar

Month	Days
Muharram	30
Safar	29
Rabi al-awwal (Rabi I)	30
Rabi al-thani (Rabi II)	29
Jumada al-awwal (Jumada I)	30
Jumada al-thani (Jumada II)	29
Rajab	30
Sha'aban	29
Ramadan	30
Shawwal	29
Dhu al-Qa'dah	30
Dhu al-Hijjah	29/30

▲ The months of the Muslim calendar.

To keep track of the days of the year, many people in the world use a calendar which divides the year into 12 months and begins on January 1. In this calendar, the Sun is used as a guide and one year is about the time it takes the Earth to move around the Sun.

But not all calendars look like this. Some calendars, for example, use the way the Moon moves across the sky as a guide. This is how the Muslim calendar works.

Each month is equal to the number of days it takes the Moon to orbit the earth. This is either 29 or 30 days.

Because the Muslim calendar has 12 shorter months, it is 11 days shorter than the common calendar. So, each of the Muslim holidays begins 11 days earlier each year.

Dates

Dates are give as CE, which means Common Era. This is the same as the Christian AD, but has no direct religious connection.

▶ In this chart, you can see how the Muslim holy days are spread around the year. You can also see how the holidays move from year to year.

MUSLIM HOLY DAYS

	2007	2008	2009	2010	2011
Ashura	Jan 20	Dec 30	Dec 19	Dec 8	Nov 27
Mawlid al-Nabi	Mar 31	Mar 20	Mar 9	Feb 26	Feb 15
Laylat al-Miraj	Sept 1	Aug 21	Aug 10	July 31	July 20
Ramadan begins	Sept 13	Sept 2	Aug 22	Aug 11	July 31
Eid al-Fitr	Oct 13	Oct 2	Sept 21	Sept 10	Aug 31
Laylat al-Qadr	Nov 5	Oct 25	Oct 14	Oct 3	Sept 22
Eid al-Adha	Dec 20	Dec 9	Nov 28	Nov 17	Nov 6

Note: All holidays begin at sundown on the day before the date given here.

7

The New Year

The Muslim calendar starts with a celebration of the beginning of Islam.

▲ On the New Year, there are worship services in the mosque.

The Muslim calendar begins with a holy day – al-Hijirah, or the New Year. This is the first day of the month of Muharram, the first month on the Muslim calendar.

The New Year holiday celebrates two things: the start of a new year; and the time that the prophet Mohammed (pbuh) left the city of Mecca for the city of Medina and started the first Islamic rule (in what is now Saudi Arabia). So, the New Year is a time to celebrate two new beginnings – the beginning of the year and the beginning of Islam.

The word **HIJIRAH** is an Arabic word that means '**EMIGRATION**' or flight, and learning the story of how Mohammed (pbuh) moved from Mecca to Medina is an important part of the New Year holiday.

▶ Most Muslims celebrate the New Year with worship services at the mosque.

The story of the Hijirah

The story begins around 1,400 years ago, in the year 622 CE. The prophet Mohammed (pbuh) had been preaching in the city of Mecca for about eight years.

At first, Mohammed (pbuh) only preached at home, to his family and friends. But as he began to preach about Islam to more and more people, the rulers of Mecca became angry with him. The rulers of Mecca worshipped many different gods, and they did not like it when Mohammed (pbuh) preached that there was only one God.

In 622, the rulers of Mecca forced Mohammed (pbuh) and his followers to leave Mecca. They fled to the city of Medina, which is about 500 km away. This escape to Medina is called the flight, or emigration (hijirah in Arabic).

The people of Medina were already familiar with the idea of one God, and after just a few years most of them had converted to Islam and become Muslims. So, the year that Mohammed (pbuh) moved (emigrated) to Medina is the start of the spread of Islam around the world.

SAUDI ARABIA

Medina

Mecca

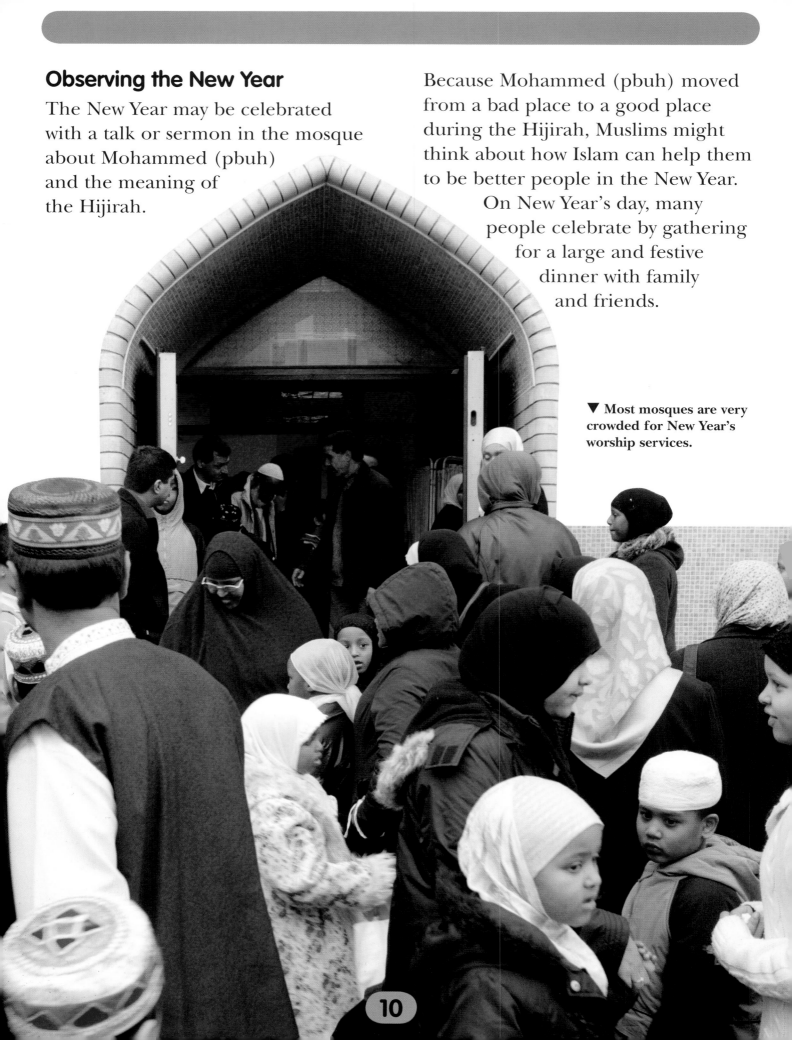

Observing the New Year

The New Year may be celebrated with a talk or sermon in the mosque about Mohammed (pbuh) and the meaning of the Hijirah.

Because Mohammed (pbuh) moved from a bad place to a good place during the Hijirah, Muslims might think about how Islam can help them to be better people in the New Year. On New Year's day, many people celebrate by gathering for a large and festive dinner with family and friends.

▼ Most mosques are very crowded for New Year's worship services.

▲ These Muslims in Turkey are sad on the holy day of Ashura because they are remembering how Imam Hussain was killed in a battle in 680 CE.

A time of sadness

In some Muslim traditions, the first ten days of the New Year are also a time to remember an event that happened in 680 CE, when the grandson of the Prophet Mohammed (pbuh), **IMAM HUSSAIN**, was killed in a battle. For these Muslims, the New Year begins a ten day period of mourning and sadness. This period is called Muharram, which is the same as the Arabic name of the month.

During this time, people gather to hear stories about how Imam Hussain and his family were killed during the battle. There may also be plays which tell the story of the battle.

On the 10th day of the month special funerals for Imam Hussain are held, and people visit mosques to pray for Hussain and his family. This holy day is called Ashura, which means 'ten'.

Some Muslims celebrate this day as the day on which God saved many prophets from their difficulties, such as Moses parting the Red Sea. Many people fast and then prepare a special meal of nine different grains.

The Prophet's birthday

This day celebrates the birthday of the prophet Mohammed (pbuh).

On the twelfth day of the third month in the Muslim calendar, many Muslims celebrate the birthday of the prophet Mohammed (pbuh), the founder of Islam. This holiday is called the Mawlid al-Nabi, or the 'festival of birth'.

Different traditions

For some Muslims, this is a happy and joyous time, when celebrations continue late into the night. For example, in Egypt, the streets are decorated with lights and banners and people stay up all night listening to religious music and watching traditional dancing.

For others, this is a quiet day simply to remember Mohammed (pbuh) and his teachings. For these people, the holiday may be celebrated with worship, talks about Islam, and community events or festivals. These may include reciting poems and singing songs that are used only at this time.

▲▶ On the prophet Mohammed's (pbuh) birthday, special songs may be sung in community celebrations.

▼ Many people compose poems that honour the prophet Mohammed (pbuh) as a way to celebrate his birthday.

Other mawlids

In some Muslim countries, additional festivals are also celebrated throughout the year to remember important Muslims. These vary from country to country. In some places, many **MAWLIDS** are celebrated each year, while in others, only the prophet Mohammed's (pbuh) mawlid is celebrated.

▲ During mawlid celebrations, songs and special types of dancing help to bring people closer to God.

Mawlid celebrations

One common way to celebrate the birthday of the prophet Mohammed (pbuh) is to listen to talks about his life and about Islam. These may take place in a mosque, or outdoors as part of a community festival.

Poems about Mohammed (pbuh) may also be recited, there may be religious music, and special religious songs may be sung.

These poems, songs and music are used only at this time. There may also be processions and other community events.

This is a happy time, but it is also a time to show respect for Mohammed (pbuh), so all of the talks, music and singing is about Mohammed (pbuh), Islam and God.

This is also a time for people to make delicious traditional food and invite friends and family members for a special festive meal. Many mosques and Muslim community organisations also have festive meals for the community at this time.

◄ All of the songs that are sung during mawlids have religious themes.

▼ Many mawlid celebrations include festive foods. This man is handing out free food during a procession in honour of the prophet Mohammed (pbuh).

The holy month of Ramadan

This holy month is a time of fasting and prayer.

Ramadan is the ninth month of the Muslim calendar. The entire month of Ramadan is a holy time in Islam.

The holy month of Ramadan celebrates the time when the Prophet Mohammed (pbuh) received his first message from God. This message included the first part of the Islamic holy scriptures, the Qur'an. So, Ramadan is a time to think about God and to thank God for the gift of the Qur'an.

▶ Ramadan celebrates the first message that Mohammed (pbuh) received from God. The entire message can be found in the Holy Qur'an (see opposite).

The story of Ramadan

Muslim tradition tells the story of how Mohammed (pbuh) was given the Muslim holy scriptures by an angel.

Throughout his life, Mohammed (pbuh) would often go into the desert, to a cave on a mountain called Mount Hira, and think about God. One day during the month of Ramadan, in the year 610 CE, the angel Gabriel came to visit him in the cave, and announced that Mohammed (pbuh) had been chosen as God's messenger. The angel also gave Mohammed (pbuh) the first part of the Qur'an.

Over the next 23 years, the angel Gabriel visited Mohammed (pbuh) many times, giving him another part of the Qur'an each time. Mohammed (pbuh) memorised the holy words and recited the messages to his followers, who also memorised them. Eventually, they were written down in a holy book – the Qur'an.

عَبَسَ وَتَوَلَّىٰ ﴿١﴾ أَن جَاءَهُ الْأَعْمَىٰ ﴿٢﴾ وَمَا يُدْرِيكَ لَعَلَّهُ يَزَّكَّىٰ ﴿٣﴾ أَوْ يَذَّكَّرُ فَتَنفَعَهُ الذِّكْرَىٰ ﴿٤﴾ أَمَّا مَنِ اسْتَغْنَىٰ ﴿٥﴾ فَأَنتَ لَهُ تَصَدَّىٰ ﴿٦﴾ وَمَا عَلَيْكَ أَلَّا يَزَّكَّىٰ ﴿٧﴾ وَأَمَّا مَن جَاءَكَ يَسْعَىٰ ﴿٨﴾ وَهُوَ يَخْشَىٰ ﴿٩﴾ فَأَنتَ عَنْهُ تَلَهَّىٰ ﴿١٠﴾ كَلَّا إِنَّهَا تَذْكِرَةٌ ﴿١١﴾ فَمَن شَاءَ ذَكَرَهُ ﴿١٢﴾ فِي صُحُفٍ مُّكَرَّمَةٍ ﴿١٣﴾ مَّرْفُوعَةٍ مُّطَهَّرَةٍ ﴿١٤﴾ بِأَيْدِي سَفَرَةٍ ﴿١٥﴾ كِرَامٍ بَرَرَةٍ ﴿١٦﴾ قُتِلَ الْإِنسَانُ مَا أَكْفَرَهُ ﴿١٧﴾ مِنْ أَيِّ شَيْءٍ خَلَقَهُ ﴿١٨﴾ مِن نُّطْفَةٍ خَلَقَهُ فَقَدَّرَهُ ﴿١٩﴾ ثُمَّ السَّبِيلَ يَسَّرَهُ ﴿٢٠﴾ ثُمَّ أَمَاتَهُ فَأَقْبَرَهُ ﴿٢١﴾ ثُمَّ إِذَا شَاءَ أَنشَرَهُ ﴿٢٢﴾ كَلَّا لَمَّا يَقْضِ مَا أَمَرَهُ ﴿٢٣﴾ فَلْيَنظُرِ الْإِنسَانُ إِلَىٰ طَعَامِهِ ﴿٢٤﴾ أَنَّا صَبَبْنَا الْمَاءَ صَبًّا ﴿٢٥﴾ ثُمَّ شَقَقْنَا الْأَرْضَ شَقًّا ﴿٢٦﴾ فَأَنبَتْنَا فِيهَا حَبًّا ﴿٢٧﴾ وَعِنَبًا وَقَضْبًا ﴿٢٨﴾ وَزَيْتُونًا وَنَخْلًا ﴿٢٩﴾ وَحَدَائِقَ غُلْبًا ﴿٣٠﴾ وَفَاكِهَةً وَأَبًّا ﴿٣١﴾ مَّتَاعًا لَّكُمْ وَلِأَنْعَامِكُمْ ﴿٣٢﴾ فَإِذَا جَاءَتِ الصَّاخَّةُ ﴿٣٣﴾ يَوْمَ يَفِرُّ الْمَرْءُ مِنْ أَخِيهِ ﴿٣٤﴾ وَأُمِّهِ وَأَبِيهِ ﴿٣٥﴾ وَصَاحِبَتِهِ وَبَنِيهِ ﴿٣٦﴾ لِكُلِّ امْرِئٍ مِّنْهُمْ يَوْمَئِذٍ شَأْنٌ يُغْنِيهِ ﴿٣٧﴾ وُجُوهٌ يَوْمَئِذٍ مُّسْفِرَةٌ ﴿٣٨﴾ ضَاحِكَةٌ مُّسْتَبْشِرَةٌ ﴿٣٩﴾ وَوُجُوهٌ يَوْمَئِذٍ عَلَيْهَا غَبَرَةٌ ﴿٤٠﴾ تَرْهَقُهَا قَتَرَةٌ ﴿٤١﴾ أُولَٰئِكَ هُمُ الْكَفَرَةُ الْفَجَرَةُ ﴿٤٢﴾

Fasting on Ramadan

During the month of Ramadan, many Muslims **FAST** (do not eat or drink) each day from sunrise to sunset.

Fasting is a way that Muslims show their devotion to God. Fasting is also a way for people to show they are grateful for all of the blessings they have received, for example, for the blessing of food – and to help them feel compassion for those who are less fortunate.

During Ramadan, families wake up very early and eat a meal before sunrise. Nothing else will be eaten or drunk until sunset. As soon as the Sun sets, the fast is broken with a light snack. One traditional snack is to eat a few dates and drink water. This is followed by the sunset prayer. This prayer can be said anywhere, but during Ramadan, many people try to say this prayer in a mosque.

After the sunset prayer, a proper meal, called **IFTAR**, is eaten. Any type of food can be eaten for iftar. During Ramadan, people often invite friends and family to share the iftar meal.

▼▶ **Many people break their fast each evening with a glass of water and a few dates. This is the way that Mohammed (pbuh) broke his fast.**

► Many families light decorative Ramadan lamps during the month as part of the celebrations. The lamps can be a reminder of the light of God.

Other ways to celebrate

Ramadan is more than a time of not eating. It is also a time to think about God and about the teachings in the Qur'an. So, Ramadan is also celebrated through worship and prayer.

There are special night-time prayers in the mosque every evening during Ramadan. In many mosques, a part of the Qur'an is read aloud each night, so that at the end of the month the entire Qur'an has been recited. These prayers are called TARAWEEH.

Another way that Muslims observe the holy time of Ramadan is by giving to charity. For example, mosques may offer free iftar meals.

Holy days during Ramadan

Although the whole month of Ramadan is a holy time, some days are especially important.

For example, according to Muslim tradition, the last ten days of Ramadan are a time when the Gates of Heaven are open and angels come to Earth to give worshippers blessings from God. This is also a time when God may forgive any bad things a person may have done.

Many Muslims spend as much of this time as they can in the mosque, praying and reading the Qur'an. Special prayers, asking God for forgiveness, are said in the mosque during this time.

▼▶ Many people try to come to the mosque for evening prayers every day during Ramadan. On the 27th night of Ramadan, many people spend the entire night in prayer in the mosque.

Holy night

The 27th night of the month of Ramadan is called Laylat al-Qadr, which means 'Night of Power'. According to Muslim tradition, this is the night on which God gave the prophet Mohammed (pbuh) the very first part of the Qur'an.

Many Muslims stay awake in the mosque or at home all night long, praying and thinking about God.

According to Muslim tradition, worshippers who pray all night long on this night will be forgiven for any bad things they may have done.

Eid al-Fitr (Feast of Breaking the Fast)

This holy day celebrates the end of the month of Ramadan and the end of fasting.

▲ Many people celebrate Ramadan by giving gifts of traditional Eid sweets.

The month of Ramadan ends with a three day holiday, called Eid al-Fitr or the Feast of Breaking the Fast. The word eid means 'feast' or 'holiday'.

During this holiday, Muslims celebrate the end of Ramadan and the end of fasting, but this is also a time to thank God for giving them the strength to fast. This is a time of joyous celebration and a chance to spend time with family and friends.

The start of the Eid

Remember that the Muslim calendar follows the Moon. So, the Eid al-Fitr holiday begins when the New Moon is seen in the night sky. This means the month of Ramadan is over and a new month has begun.

On the first day of the holiday, everyone gets up very early in the morning to go to the mosque for worship services. These services are held about 80 minutes after sunrise.

After the morning worship service, families go home or gather together at the mosque to eat a celebratory breakfast. This is the first daytime meal Muslims will have eaten in a month.

▼ These sweet cheese pastries are popular Eid treats.

▼ During Eid, there are many community celebrations and festive meals.

▲ These people are praying during an outdoor service at the beginning of the Eid al-Fitr.

Celebrating Eid al-Fitr

Eid al-Fitr is a time of celebration and of sharing. So, during the holiday, people spend a lot of time visiting friends and family.

Outdoor festivals or fêtes are another popular way to celebrate the holiday. These may take place at mosques or other places and often include food and games. In some places, there may also be special worship services out of doors, and processions through the streets.

Some Muslim communities also put up coloured lights in the streets at this time, and families may decorate their houses with coloured lights and banners.

One tradition is to give small gifts of money to children. When someone visits during the holiday, they give a very small amount of brand new notes or coins to the children of the house.

Another tradition is to give special sweets made just for the holiday to friends and family. These sweets are a reminder of the sweetness of the holiday. In fact, sometimes this holiday is called the 'sweet eid' or 'sweet holiday'.

▼ Some families visit the cemetery at this time to remember their ancestors and family members who have died.

► This community Eid al-Fitr celebration includes traditional foods like rice with meat and dates filled with almonds, walnuts and candied peel.

Most Muslims also give money to charity, which is used to make sure that everyone can celebrate the Eid with a nice meal, sweets and new clothes.

For family and friends who live far away, one modern custom is to send 'Happy Eid al-Fitr' cards.

Eid al-Adha (Feast of the Sacrifice)

This holiday celebrates an important event in the Qur'an.

This holiday, which begins on the tenth day of the last month of the Muslim year, honours an event that happened in Biblical times and is written about in both the Bible and the Qur'an. This holiday lasts for three days.

The story of the Eid al-Adha

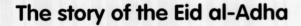

The story of the Eid al-Adha begins with Abraham. Jews, Muslims and Christians all believe that Abraham was one of the founders of the Jewish religion, and one of the first people to believe in one God.

Abraham's people worshipped many gods, but Abraham came to believe that the entire universe was the work of a single God, and he began to teach this belief to others.

One night, as he slept, Abraham had a dream. In the dream, God asked Abraham to sacrifice, or kill, his son Ishmail.

Abraham became very sad at this, but he felt sure that God had given him an order and that he had to obey it. First of all, he talked to his son:

"My dear son, I have seen in a dream that I should sacrifice you. My heart is heavy."

Abraham's son loved God. So he told his father: "Dear father, if God has ordered it, then you must obey, so sacrifice me. Do not be sad; with God's help, I shall be brave."

So, Abraham and Ishmail went into the desert. On their way, the devil tried three times to convince Abraham to disobey God and not sacrifice his beloved son. But Abraham and Ishmail did not listen to the devil and chased him away each time.

Finally, full of sorrow, Abraham prepared to kill his son. But at the last moment, God stopped him and gave him a male sheep (ram) to sacrifice instead. Abraham and Ishmail had proven their obedience to God. Muslims celebrate this every year with the Eid al-Adha.

▲ The Eid al-Adha marks
the end of the pilgrimage, or
HAJJ, the time when Muslims
visit the holy site of the Ka'ba
(shown here) in Mecca, Saudi
Arabia. The Ka'ba was first
built by Adam as the first
place to worship God, and
was later rebuilt by Abraham.

Celebrating in the mosque

On the first day of the Eid al-Adha, there are special worship services in the mosque.

The worship services usually include a sermon, or talk, about the meaning and importance of this holiday. During prayers, Muslims remember the way that Abraham was willing to sacrifice his son to God, and how God rewarded Abraham's obedience by letting him sacrifice a ram instead.

After worship services, everyone stands up to hug and greet one another. The traditional greeting is 'Eid Mubarak', which means 'Holiday Blessings'.

▶ Worship services may end with hugs and greetings.

28

Sacrifice on the Eid al-Adha

To remember how God let Abraham sacrifice a sheep instead of his son, it is traditional for each Muslim family to sacrifice a ram or other animal at the beginning of the holiday. One-third of the meat is kept for the family, one-third is given to friends or relatives and one-third is given to charity.

In modern times, people do not kill the sheep themselves. Instead, they may have a Muslim butcher kill the animal and prepare the meat. Or, instead of killing an animal, some families give money to charity. They give as much money as one sheep is worth. The money may be used to provide meals and new clothes for poor Muslims, so that everyone can celebrate the holiday of Eid al-Adha.

Eid celebrations

Eid is a happy time for Muslims, when they remember how important it is to make sacrifices for God, such as giving up bad habits and keeping God's rules. It is also a time for sharing and friendship between neighbours, friends and families. People visit each other's homes and enjoy festive meals.

◀ During worship services on Eid al-Adha there may be talks about the importance of obedience to God and the meaning of the Eid al-Adha.

Holy nights

There are other holy times throughout the Muslim year. Three of the most important are celebrated at night.

The night of power

This is the first of the three special nights in the Islamic calendar. This holiday happens on the 27th day of Ramadan. In Arabic it is called Laylat al-Qadr. According to Muslim tradition, this is the night on which God gave the prophet Mohammed (pbuh) the very first part of the Qur'an.

You can read more about this holy night on page 16.

The night of repentance

This night takes place on the fifteenth night of the eighth month of the Muslim calendar (Sha'aban). In Arabic it is called Shabi-barat.

Repentance means 'to feel bad for doing something wrong' and according to Muslim tradition, on this night God forgives people who have done something wrong. So, many Muslims spend this night in fasting, prayer and worship, and ask God for forgiveness for past sins and for blessings. The next day is spent fasting.

The night journey

This night remembers when God brought Mohammed (pbuh) up to Heaven and gave him the daily prayers. It is celebrated on the 27th day of the seventh month of the Muslim calendar (Rajab). In Arabic this night is called Laylat Al-Isra wa Al-Miraj.

According to Muslim tradition, on this night, the prophet Mohammed (pbuh) was woken up by the angel Gabriel. The angel gave Mohammed (pbuh) a heavenly winged horse, called Buraq, who carried him to Jerusalem. There, in the Mosque of Al Aqsa, Mohammed (pbuh) led all of God's prophets in prayer.

From Jerusalem, Mohammed (pbuh) climbed a staircase up to Heaven, where he met with prophets such as Abraham, Moses and Jesus.

Finally, Mohammed (pbuh) came to the Throne of God and met God Himself. Here, God gave Mohammed (pbuh) the daily prayers and told him to have all Muslims recite them 50 times each day.

Mohammed (pbuh) told God that this will be too hard and asked God to reduce the number of prayer times to five each day. God agreed. This is the origin of the practice in which all Muslims must recite the daily prayers five times each day.

Muslims celebrate this event simply, with poems, worship and prayer in the mosque.

Index

Curriculum Visions

Curriculum Visions is a registered trademark of Atlantic Europe Publishing Company Ltd.

Atlantic Europe Publishing

First published in 2007 by Atlantic Europe Publishing Company Ltd Copyright © 2007 Earthscape

The right of Lisa Magloff to be identified as the author of this work has been asserted by her in accordance with the Copyright, Designs and Patents Act 1988.

Author
Lisa Magloff, MA

Religious Adviser
Iqbal Turk, chairman, the Sunni Muslim Association, London.

Senior Designer
Adele Humphries, BA

Acknowledgements
The publishers would like to thank everyone at the Sunni Muslim Association, London; London Islamic Cultural Society and mosque.

Photographs
The Earthscape Picture Library, except: (c=centre, t=top, b=bottom, l=left, r=right) page 11 *Alamy*; pages 18, 19, 21 (background), 22, 25c, 26–27, 30–31 *ShutterStock*.

Illustrations
David Woodroffe

Designed and produced by
Earthscape

Printed in China by
WKT Company Ltd

Muslim holy days
– Curriculum Visions
A CIP record for this book is available from the British Library
ISBN: 978 1 86214 506 1

This product is manufactured from sustainable managed forests. For every tree cut down at least one more is planted.

Dedicated Web Site
There's more about other great Curriculum Visions packs and a wealth of supporting information on world religions and other subjects at our dedicated web site:
www.CurriculumVisions.com

Clap Yo' Hands

(from *Oh, Kay!*)

Music by George Gershwin

Spirited (but sustained)

Concerto In F
(1st Movement Theme)

Music by George Gershwin
Arranged by Matthew King

15

Embraceable You

(from *Girl Crazy*)

Music by George Gershwin

A Foggy Day

(from *A Damsel In Distress*)

Music by George Gershwin

Moderately, with a strong beat

I Got Rhythm

(from *Girl Crazy*)

Music by George Gershwin

I Loves You, Porgy

(from *Porgy And Bess*)

Music by George Gershwin
Arranged by Jerry Lanning

Freely

Andantino molto espressivo

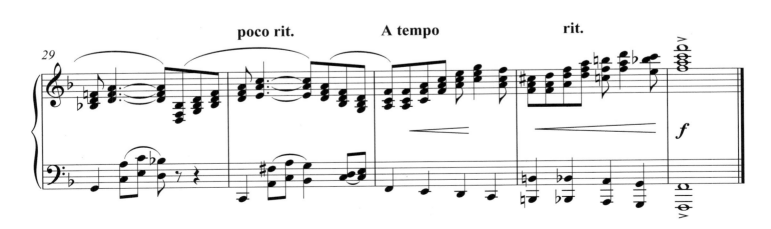

poco rit.   A tempo   rit.

I'll Build A Stairway To Paradise

(from *George White's Scandals Of 1922*)

Music by George Gershwin

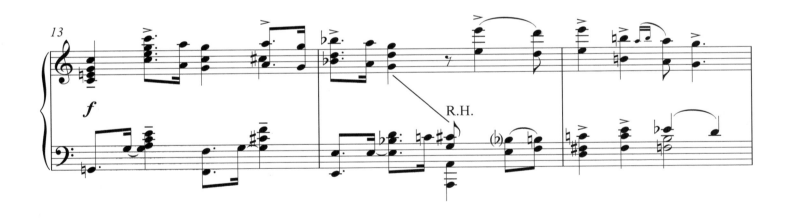

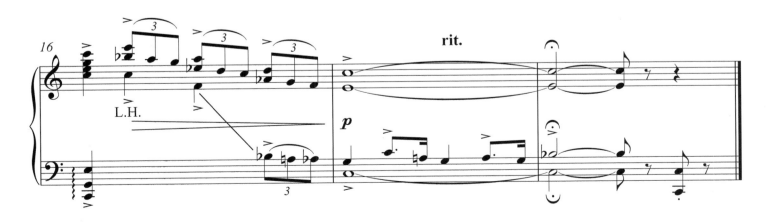

It Ain't Necessarily So

(from *Porgy And Bess*)

Music by George Gershwin

Slow blues tempo

Fascinating Rhythm

(from *Lady, Be Good*)

Music by George Gershwin

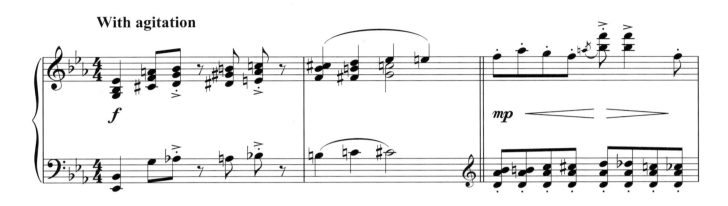

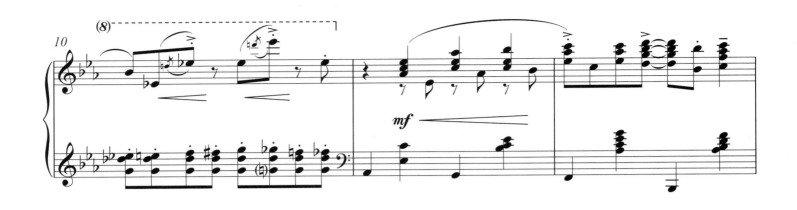

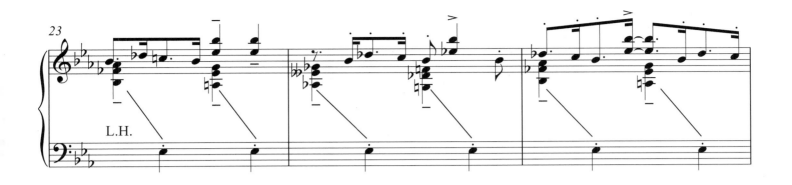

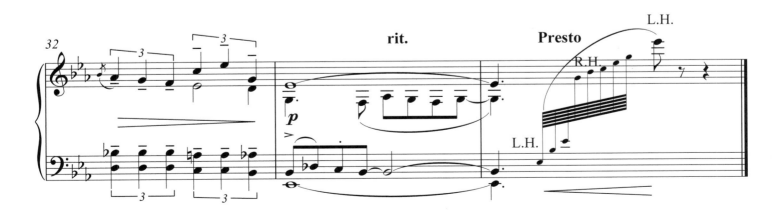

Let's Call The Whole Thing Off

(from *Shall We Dance?*)

Music by George Gershwin
Arranged by Matthew King

Love Walked In

(from *The Goldwyn Follies*)

Music by George Gershwin
Arranged by Jerry Lanning

A tempo

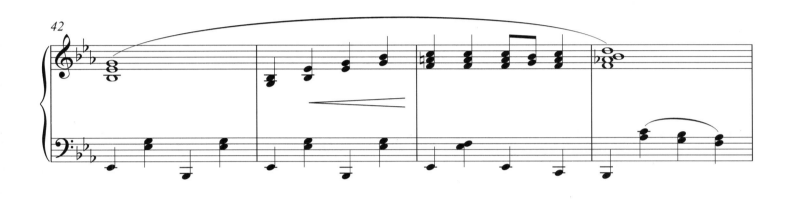

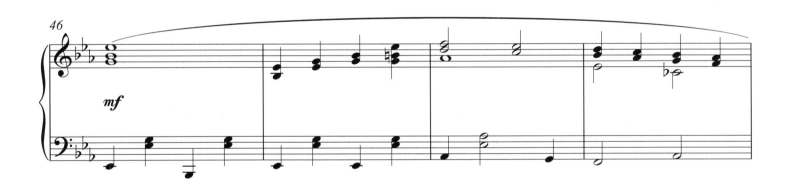

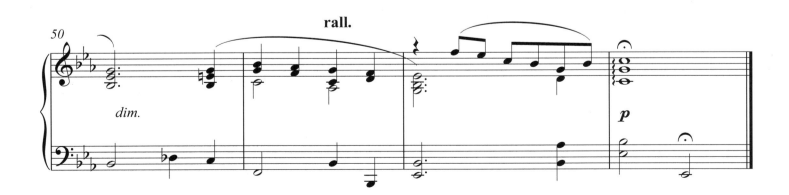

Nice Work If You Can Get It

(from *A Damsel In Distress*)

Music by George Gershwin

Moderately

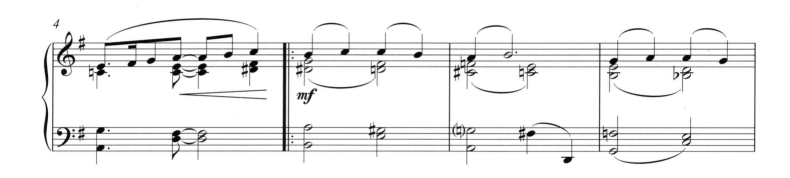

Oh, Lady, Be Good

(from *Lady, Be Good*)

Music by George Gershwin

Rather slow (with humour)

ff

il basso marcato

poco a poco cresc.

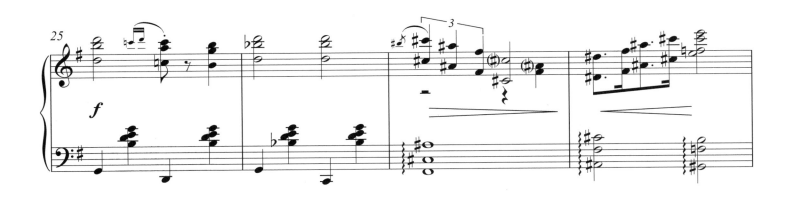

f

Prélude No.1

(from *Three Préludes For Piano*)

Music by George Gershwin

Prélude No.2

(from *Three Préludes For Piano*)

Music by George Gershwin

Andante con moto e poco rubato (♩ = 88)

Prélude No.3

(from *Three Préludes For Piano*)

Music by George Gershwin

The Man I Love

(from *Lady, Be Good*)

Music by George Gershwin

Slowly, with expression

Rhapsody In Blue
(Opening Themes)

Music by George Gershwin
Arranged by Jerry Lanning

Molto moderato (♩ = 80)

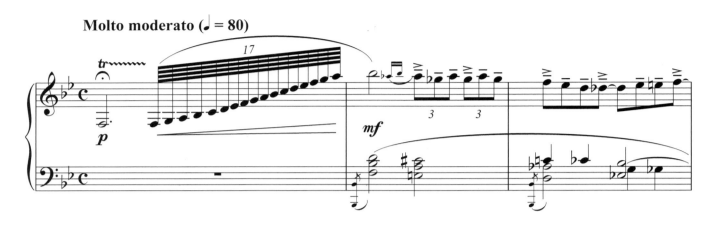

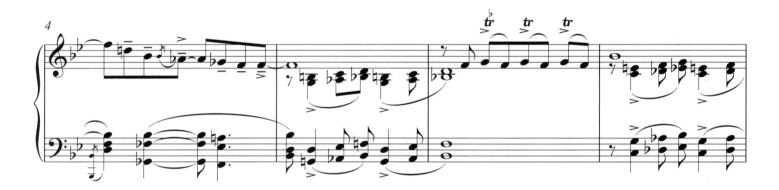

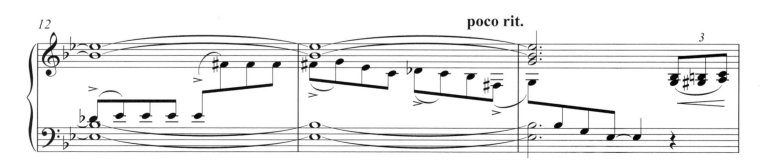

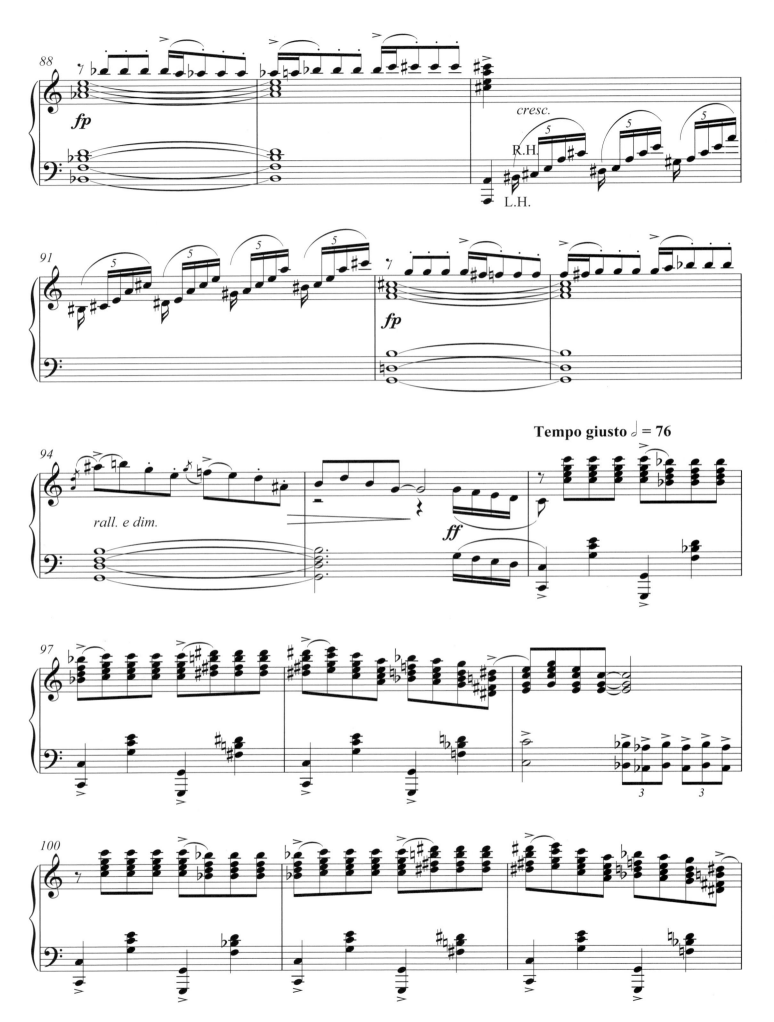

69

Rhapsody In Blue
(Slow Theme)

Music by George Gershwin
Arranged by Jerry Lanning

Andantino moderato

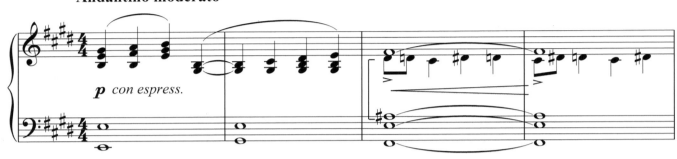

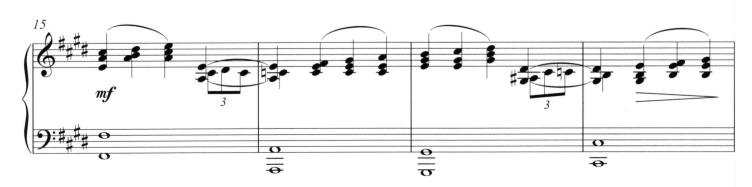

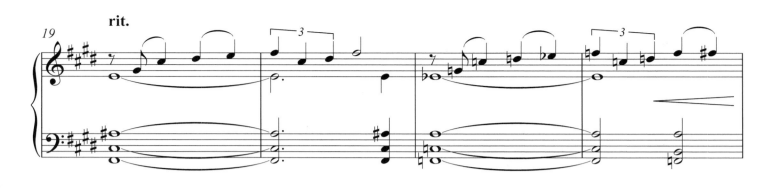

'S Wonderful

(from *Funny Face*)

Music by George Gershwin

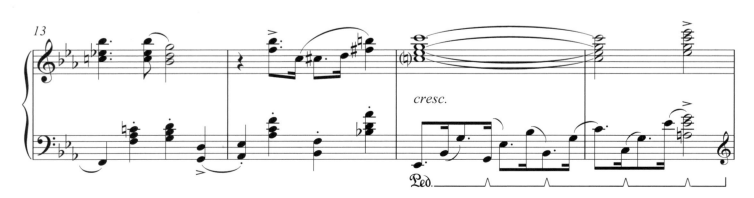

Someone To Watch Over Me

(from *Oh, Kay!*)

Music by George Gershwin

Arranged by Jerry Lanning

Moderato

Strike Up The Band

(from *Strike Up The Band*)

Music by George Gershwin

Swanee

(from *Capitol Revue*)

Music by George Gershwin
Arranged by Matthew King

Ragtime tempo ♩ = 110

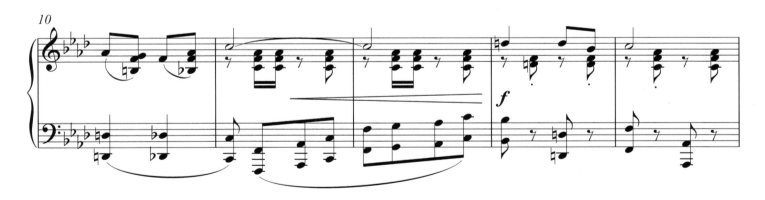

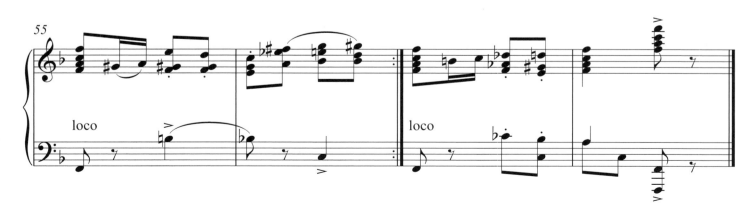

85

Summertime

(from *Porgy And Bess*)

Music by George Gershwin

Sweet And Low Down

(from *Tip-Toes*)

Music by George Gershwin

They All Laughed

(from *Shall We Dance?*)

Music by George Gershwin
Arranged by Matthew King

With swing ♩ = 120

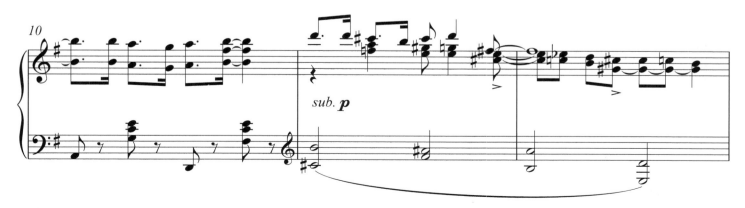

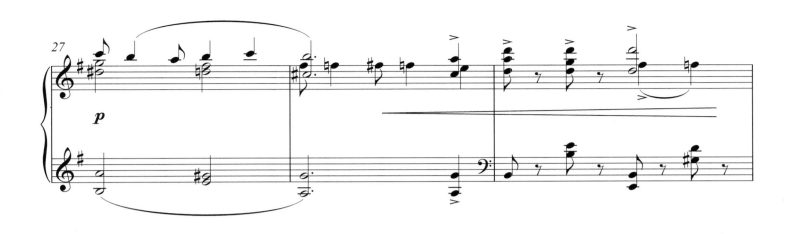

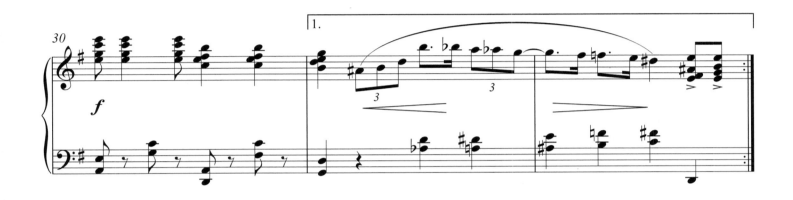

They Can't Take That Away From Me

(from *Shall We Dance?*)

Music by George Gershwin

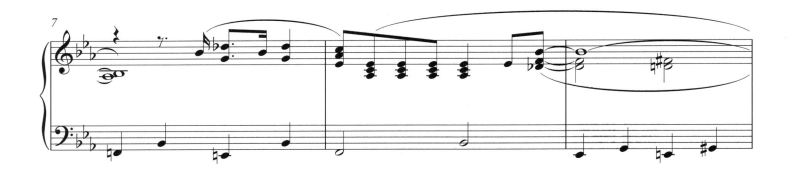